Creating Character Emotions

Creating Character Emotions

ANN HOOD

STORY PRESS

CINCINNATI, OHIO

Creating Character Emotions. Copyright © 1998 by Ann Hood. Printed and bound in the United States of America. All rights reserved. No part of this book may be reproduced in any form or by any electronic or mechanical means including information storage and retrieval systems without permission in writing from the publisher, except by a reviewer, who may quote brief passages in a review. Published by Story Press, an imprint of F&W Publications, Inc., 1507 Dana Avenue, Cincinnati, Ohio 45207. (800) 289-0963. First edition.

Story Press Books are available from your local bookstore or direct from the publisher.

02 01 00 99 98   5 4 3 2 1

Library of Congress Cataloging-in-Publication Data

Hood, Ann.
   Creating character emotions / Ann Hood.
      p.   cm.
   Includes index.
   ISBN 1-884910-33-5 (alk. paper)
   1. Authorship. 2. Fiction—Technique. 3. Characters and characteristics. I.
   Title.
PN218.H66   1997
808.3'97—dc21   97-31296
                                                                CIP

Designed by Clare Finney

For my teachers:

Warren Smith
William Decker
Nicholas Delbanco
and
Lloyd and Gloria Hood

CONTENTS

HOW DID YOU KNOW?

When I moved last summer, I came across a box filled with various versions of the syllabus I use when I teach fiction writing. In one way or another, each version covered the same topics: how to get started, how to create setting, how to plot the action, how to sustain dramatic tension, how to revise. Sometimes I added a lesson on writing strong dialogue; sometimes we worked on creating believable characters.

But none of these carefully planned classes discussed how to render character emotions. Yet this book is devoted entirely to doing just that. And I believe this is some of the most important information you can use as a fiction writer. So was I remiss in not including this topic on a syllabus in the past ten years of teaching creative writing? It would certainly seem that way, considering how vital writing believable emotions is to good fiction.

However, the truth is that the lessons about rendering character emotions were taught every time class met. Emotions affect every other element of fiction—dialogue, action, character development, plot, theme. "Our feelings," Audre Lorde wrote in *Black Women Writers at Work*, "are our most genuine paths to knowledge." The same can be said for the emotions we render in our fiction: When written well and convincingly, they lead us to more genuine characters who act and speak and think in a richer way. Emotions lead us to more believable plot twists and turns, enhance dramatic tension, help to illustrate themes. In short, they inform every aspect of our fiction.

The importance of writing strong and honest emotions was made clear to me when Bantam Books was about to publish my first novel, *Somewhere off the Coast of Maine*. The book explores the lives of three women who were friends in college in the '60s by examining what has happened to them since then and where they are now.

Although the book is not autobiographical, each character has a small piece of me in her.

For example, when I was a teenager I believed I would be more popular and more accepted if I wore contact lenses. At the time, everyone wore round, wire-rimmed glasses like John Lennon's. My eyesight is so bad that my heavy lenses popped out of the wire frames every afternoon during last period. I carried a set of jeweler's screwdrivers in my purse for the sole purpose of putting my glasses back together—one more thing that labelled me as weird. Much of my teen angst was epitomized by those glasses. When I walked out of the optometrist's office, teary-eyed and blinking like a caution light from my new contact lenses, I was certain everyone would see me as a new person.

When I wanted to create an adolescent character who feels out of place in her world, I thought of my own teenaged self sitting in social studies at John F. Deering Junior High, carefully screwing my glasses together, pretending not to be humiliated. But the character I came up with wasn't me; her problems and her environment were uniquely her own. Still, by revisiting my own painful experience, I was able to create one for her that felt right.

Rebekah, the daughter of one of the three women, is convinced she is unpopular because she has a big nose. And she believes that a nose job will fix everything in her life.

> Rebekah had decided that the source of her humiliation was her nose. Despite her mother's donation of carob brownies to the junior high bake sale and her father's refusal to pay income tax and the organic garden in their yard—despite everything—Rebekah decided that it was indeed her nose that placed her in the caste of Untouchable at school. Her nose was large and sprawling, like her house. And it had a bump on it. If it were small and smooth, Rebekah thought, life would be all right.

Rebekah gets a nose job by stealing money from her parents, but of course it doesn't change anyone's opinion about her at school.

When I went to Bantam to meet all of the people involved with the book's publication, I noticed that everybody I met studied my face a bit too carefully. The usual fears crept in—I had something in my teeth or coming out of my nose or a new blemish on my cheek. Until one woman blurted, "Why! You never had a nose job!" Stunned, I blurted back, "Of course not!" "But," she said, "how did you know what it was like?"

How did you know?

If you render character emotion effectively and honestly, that is the question your readers will ask. "How did you know what it was like to have a child when you don't have one yourself?" "How did you know what it felt like to be so ill if you have been healthy?" "How did you know?"

Perhaps it sounds simple. Aha! All I need to do is match up an emotional state of my own with one I want my character to have, change a few details, and I've captured that emotion perfectly. As you know by now if you've been practicing the craft of fiction, it's never that easy. If it were, we wouldn't leave so many stories unconvinced by how a character acted, or how the plot moved. We wouldn't be left emotionally cold.

What follows on these pages are ways to break through to writing effective, authentic emotions in our fiction. We will explore the ranges of dozens of emotions, the pitfalls in writing them, hints to writing them well. We will look at examples—good and bad—of how other writers have accomplished the task. And, finally, there are exercises for you to practice rendering specific emotions for your characters.

This book can become a handbook of sorts, a companion that will help you think about the importance of emotions in fiction as well as a guide for you in writing. Because of the rippling effect of emotions in fiction—the way they help to create character, setting, theme, and plot—this is a book you can turn to often. It will, I hope, lead to a reader asking you, "How did you know?"

PART ONE

WRITING ABOUT EMOTION

It always strikes me as funny that in our daily lives we pass through a whole spectrum of emotions and show them in many ways, some obvious and some subtle, yet in our fiction we often have trouble moving our characters through emotions effectively. I think of this as the curse of writing like a writer. Sometimes we get a tone or a voice in our head and we decide that is how good writers sound.

In a class I took at New York University with E.L. Doctorow, he once mentioned that the curse of his generation was trying to write like Hemingway and that the curse of our generation was trying to write like Raymond Carver. When I got home that night and looked at my own stories that I had been struggling to get right, I saw that Doctorow had hit on an important lesson. I *was* trying to sound like Carver. And at other points in my life, I tried to sound like F. Scott Fitzgerald or Flannery O'Connor or the latest *New Yorker* story. In other words, I was trying to write like a writer.

When we copy a writerly voice, we put up a barrier between us and the emotions of our characters. As a result, the readers get filtered versions of emotion instead of real interpretations and an honest rendering of them. Please don't misunderstand me: There is much to be gained from reading and admiring another writer's work. In fact, it is a necessary part of being a writer. I agree with Saul Bellow who said, "A writer is a reader moved to emulation." However, we must also be able to let go of that writer's voice, or of the voice of that nebulous writer type—the gray-haired man in a tweed coat, the woman in a flowing white dress—whose writerly voice haunts our own work.

So my first piece of advice is to write like yourself. Until you do that, you will not be able to evoke emotion—and therefore character—effectively. Arguably the most important thing a writer can do is get readers to feel emotions. You might believe instead that conveying ideas in fiction is more important. However, I agree with Janet Burroway who, in her classic book *Writing Fiction*, argues that the ideas must be experienced through or with the characters; they must be *felt* or the fiction will fail.

Your goal, then, is to have your characters and your readers feel the necessary emotions, to believe in them, so your ideas will be conveyed convincingly and your fiction will succeed. Put aside the writerly voice. You are now ready to write like the most important writer you will need to create convincing emotions: yourself.

FICTION VS. REAL LIFE

It is important to remember fiction is not real life. We can't rely on easy emotional associations or true stories to render fictional emotional truth; it will inevitably sound false. I remember a student of mine who reported events exactly as they happened and called it fiction. One story in particular was about a young couple breaking up. The boy was heartbroken. Each of them said things that were at times meant to be sad, at times filled with despair or jealousy, love or resignation. In between the dialogue was plenty of silence. The story, rather than leaving the reader heartbroken like its main character, was flat and inauthentic. "But this is what happened to me!" the writer said. "And I am heartbroken!" "I believe you," I said. "Now I have to believe that your character is heartbroken."

A brief journey through my own emotional day feels like this: I overslept and so was worried that I wouldn't get my son to school on time. I did, but on the way home the road was closed and I felt confused about how to proceed. By the time I found my way home, I couldn't do any of the things I needed to get done before I took my father to a doctor's appointment so I ended up guiltily wasting time at a local cafe. However, the time to myself made me feel quite happy. My father's appointment went well and we both were more hopeful about his recovery than we had been, so we went out for a celebratory lunch at which we both felt a lot of love. When I got home and finally settled down to my computer, my daughter started crying, which irritated me. She settled down for a nap and here I am. It's just three o'clock in the afternoon and I've only told you the major emotions I experienced so far.

But if I were a character in a story, these emotions would have to hold more weight. For example, it would be more important to understand how I reached a hopeful emotional place with my father's illness. I could juxtapose this doctor's visit with one several months ago that left me in despair.

Also, emotions shouldn't be as flat in fiction as they can be in real life. In a story a writer must ask more of emotions. Was the confusion I felt at getting lost this morning important? Why did it matter? What does it say about me, the character? What does it reveal? Perhaps in life it mattered—I had things to do, after all—but in fiction we need to gauge the impact of action against our characters' emotional lives. If confusion in getting lost is only in a story because it sounds real, then don't use it. It has to be important in the fictional life of your character.

Amy Hempel addresses this question of fiction vs. truth in her story "The Harvest." The first half of the story is about a young woman who gets badly hurt in a car accident on her way to dinner with a married man; the last half of the story is the writer telling the reader which events were true and which were made up, and why: "The man of a week, whose motorcycle it was, was not a married man. But when you thought he had a wife, wasn't I liable to do anything? And didn't I have it coming?"

What a good example of demonstrating how a writer manipulates her characters' emotional lives to render certain emotions in the reader. Hempel wanted the reader to think the young woman deserved what she got. Hempel states, "I leave a lot out when I tell the truth. The same when I write a story."

The second important thing you need to do, then, is to separate life from fiction. You need to step into the life of your story, to leave out a lot and still tell the truth.

HOW TO DO IT WRONG

Even after you've managed to close out the voices of those "real" writers who haunt you and to enter your characters' fictional world, there are still a lot of common problems in portraying emotions in fiction. Identifying these problems helps us to avoid them. In fact, after you've read these and thought about them, you'll be surprised how often you'll find them, not just in your own work but in the work of other writers too.

The Cliché Trap

How easy it is to say that someone is "green with envy," or is so nervous she has "butterflies in her stomach." It's much more difficult to find a fresh way to evoke jealousy or anxiety or any emotion.

One of the problems with this is that clichés simply fall out of our heads and onto the paper. We don't even know it's happening. I remember being at a baseball game with a friend who pointed to a red-faced man walking toward us and said, "His face looks like a boiled ham." What a perfect simile! Not only did it describe the man's face, but ten years later I still remember it. To write one that perfect would take a lot of time. But to write "red as a beet" takes no time and no thought. The same is true with emotions. We have to be alert, like my friend, and reach beyond the obvious cliché.

In her book *The Passionate, Accurate Story*, Carol Bly suggests writing the second thing that comes to your mind rather than the first. Her point is that clichés are always at the forefront of our minds, and therefore are usually what we think of first. But are they effective in our writing? When Bly pushed her students to describe the drab classroom they were sitting in, after they'd used all the obvious descriptions, one of them wrote: "No one ever fell in love in this room."

I think we have to be even more meticulous in our fresh descriptions of emotions. It is easier to forgive "hair as yellow as wheat" than "as happy as a clam." After all, the emotional lives of our characters are the key to our whole story. We must always search for that "boiled ham" description, the one that jumps out at the readers, fits perfectly and stays with them long after the story has ended.

Lack of Specificity

Sometimes it is laziness that keeps a writer from doing what Flannery O'Connor called "painting a picture with words." But often this comes from the writer's own insecurity about where the character should be emotionally at this point of the story. The writer knows the character should feel *something*. But what? Instead of considering the plot of the story and the character's own emotional place, the writer relies on a nonspecific emotion and hopes the reader fills in the blanks.

In my novel *Places to Stay the Night*, I had the most trouble with the main character of Libby. She just wasn't convincing enough. I knew from the start that Libby is restless and unhappy enough to leave her husband and their two children and go to California. But I lost her authenticity when she got there. I wasn't sure myself how she felt about leaving her family behind. I had her acting out a lot of emotions in the secret hope that a reader might be able to figure out the very thing I couldn't: What did Libby feel once she acted on her other emotions?

It wasn't until I forced out significant details—Where did she work when she got there? Did she make any friends? What did she want from the move?—that I could start to understand her emotional life and to depict it convincingly. Here is an example of what Libby did there and how she felt.

> For her second acting class, Libby wore the electric blue spandex dress. An actress has to be versatile, she'd read. She wanted her teacher, Carl, to see every side of her, how much of a chameleon she could be. When she walked in, the two young blondes in the class glanced at each other. She hated them. They weren't even twenty-one, and they always wore tight black things. They had too much hair, gobs of it. And smooth flawless skin. Their names were Heather and Ashley. Libby decided, as she took her place, that they looked like everybody else, nothing special, just two more California girls. In a way, she thought, she felt bad for them.

The emotional truth here is that Libby is as unhappy in California as she was back in Massachusetts. She just isn't ready to admit it. She has discovered that there are a lot of younger, prettier girls in California and she feels jealous. Notice how the concrete details help the reader understand those emotions. Libby has on a "blue spandex dress"; the other women are wearing "tight black things."

Remember, this is Libby's point of view, so when she notices their "gobs" of hair and "smooth flawless skin," it's important to her emotional state of mind. She tries to convince herself her jealousy is really sympathy—they're not special, they look like everyone else and she actually feels bad for them. But through the specific details, the reader sees that Libby isn't feeling sympathy at all.

How much more effective these concrete details make this scene than if Libby had simply walked into her acting class and noticed the two blonde women there. Even vague descriptions might have led the reader to believe she admired them or that she was happy with herself and her life. Or the reader could simply have been left confused. Think of concrete details as emotional traffic signs, leading the reader to the right place.

Ambiguity

Ambiguity occurs when the writer does not trust her own experience with emotions enough and therefore ignores what it *really* feels like to be sad or in love or angry. A hefty part of writing is being able to explore our own inner lives, to tap into our own emotions and histories, to revisit things that perhaps are unpleasant, like my days as the ninth-grade weirdo. It is this self-exploration that led a student of mine to announce at the end of class, "I signed up for Creative Writing and got Therapy 101 instead!"

If you cannot or will not do some emotional homework, chances are you will create characters who are emotionally ambiguous. Such characters force the reader to look elsewhere in the story for clues to emotional clarification. Those clues should rest within the character. When they don't, your reader will either misunderstand the story or feel confused by it.

One way we fall into ambiguity is by labelling an emotion rather than honestly exploring it. You can avoid this by studying a model from literature. Who is one of your favorite characters? What is his emotional journey? How does the writer take you along without falling into ambiguity? You will see that the character was created without emotional shortcuts or cryptic language to label his emotional self. Clarity and honesty brought this character to life, and that is how you will create believable emotional lives for your characters.

Not Trusting Your Characters

There are times when the writer doesn't trust the characters enough and this leads to a different set of problems. For one, there can be a lack of consistency. On page 3 the character is mourning his dead wife and on page 4 he's happily shopping for a new pair of jeans, and there is no emotional journey between the two experiences. This leads the reader, of course, to not believing in the story's emotional authenticity. Characters have to work to move from grief to happiness.

Conversely, a writer who doesn't trust the characters enough can write a character who is *too* consistent, who strikes the same note too often, such as a character who is only portrayed as angry or happy. Aristotle says a character should be "consistently inconsistent"; that is important to remember. Consistently inconsistent does not mean characters jump from emotion to emotion recklessly but rather that they believably move from one emotion to the next.

Remember my character Libby? In a way, it takes the entire novel to move her from the unhappy housewife who leaves her family on page 1 to the resigned woman who returns to them on page 275. She moves from hope and excitement to loneliness and even despair before she matures emotionally.

Characters should have a range of emotion to give them depth and complexity. Otherwise, we end up with fiction filled with stereotypes, flat characters moving through an unbelievable world. Had Libby felt the jealousy I showed in the passage above and immediately turned to despair, she would not have been successfully rendered. That jealousy was just one step on an emotional ladder your characters should climb, emotional rung by emotional rung.

HOW TO DO IT RIGHT

The best fiction takes characters through not just an external journey, but an emotional journey too. As a writer, you do need a bit of "Therapy 101" to help your characters along their own emotional travels. But don't confuse emotional truth with autobiography. You must first give your characters full lives of their own. Edna O'Brien said of Chekhov: "He does not write—he breathes life off the page." Giving your characters authentic, believable emotions is the best way I know to breathe life into them and off the page.

Imagine the characters from literature whom you most believed emotionally. I think of Willa Cather's archbishop, Fitzgerald's Gatsby, Updike's Rabbit, Tolstoy's Anna Karenina. From my childhood I still remember the emotional impact of Jo March from *Little Women*; from adolescence it is Herman Wouk's Marjorie Morningstar. My father likes Tony Hillerman's detective Joe Leaphorn. My husband likes Einstein as he appears in Alan Lightman's *Einstein's Dreams*.

All of these characters have both emotional breath and emotional breadth. They live on long after you've finished the book. Can you create characters who are as emotionally developed? Can you move a character through hope to despair in the way Fitzgerald moves Jay Gatsby?

You don't need to be a literary genius, or even wildly successful, to render emotions effectively. But you do have to work at it. By now you have shut out those other writers' voices, you have successfully separated "real life" from fictional life, and you have considered the common pitfalls writers encounter when writing emotions. It's time to look at what you can do to get it right so your characters breathe off the page too.

Your Emotional Time Line

Conjuring your own emotional memories will certainly help you create emotional lives for your characters, as I did with Rebekah, my teen-ager from *Somewhere off the Coast of Maine* who believes her big nose is the cause of her loneliness. Making your own emotional time line will help you do the same for your characters.

Let's look at Rebekah and her nose job again and how my emotional life informed hers. I could say that mine began with a longing to be accepted. My sadness at being excluded from others led to my desire for a change (contact lenses). When I was still excluded, I felt disappointed and confused. But eventually these emotions led to a positive emotion—satisfaction—when I finally grew past the need to be accepted and made friends with the other "Untouchables."

After revisiting my own emotional time line, I could create a believable one for Rebekah, whose longing and sadness mirrored mine. For example, I showed her disappointment: "She sacrificed everything for this day and it was all for nothing. Tomorrow she would don her patched jeans and bicycle to school like before. It didn't matter. Her nose was different, but everything else was still the same."

At the end of *Somewhere off the Coast of Maine*, Rebekah has a boyfriend and a group of her own friends; she is even happy: "Rebekah had gone so long without friends that she didn't mind that these two weren't part of Sally Perkins' clique. In fact, she liked having her own group, where she was the important one."

It's important to remind yourself that I am not Rebekah. In a way we share an emotional life but all the props are different: She is the daughter of two hippie potters, I'm the daughter of Depression-era, white-collar parents; her mother is critically ill; she has a younger brother, the list goes on and on, all the way to the fact that she's a vegetarian. These external facts do matter. They help create the character of Rebekah and shape her emotions and her reactions to "the havoc they wreak." Our emotional lives only overlap enough to help me convince you, the reader, of authenticity.

Fresh Language

This kind of emotional work is only one way you can bring emotional truth to your fiction. There are other technical strategies you can use too. I've already mentioned Carol Bly's advice about writing the *second* thing you think of. But it's worth repeating here and to yourself, over and over. In my classes I refer to this as the Cliché Police and induct all of my students into the force. You can't be too vigilant in your attempts to overcome emotional clichés.

Fresh language and images rather than tired clichés force you—and your reader—to see emotions in a different light. How much better to say, as Susan Taylor Chehak does in her novel *Smithereens*, "I could feel the awkward, scared tumble of my heartbeat" than to say "My heart pounded."

Clichés like this one are a kind of emotional shorthand; they do the work for the writer. Or so the writer thinks. When we read a writer who relies on such emotional shorthand, we don't trust what that writer is trying to say. How can someone who tries to get away with a pounding heart know anything new or enlightening about fear?

One of my favorite clichés is one tear rolling down a cheek. Not only am I not sure if it's physically possible to produce just one tear, but the image is so overused it is now almost comical. A shorthand for sadness? Perhaps. But more likely it shows a writer's unwillingness or inability to work at rendering real emotion.

However, the reason we have read about so many hearts pounding is because there is some morsel of truth in that image. The other night, alone in our big old Victorian house, I thought I heard someone walking around downstairs. My heart did pound, but to say it that way is to cheat the reader and the emotion. That is why pushing past the cliché—using it, in a way—can be effective. If we've read "my heart pounded" enough for it to be the cliché for fear, how can we use that image more effectively? Chehak's "awkward, scared tumble" does just that: It builds on the cliché and creates something fresh.

The Power of Suggestion

Much emotional work can be done by suggestion. Remember how one pitfall was the problem of stating a character was sad without showing how he wore that sadness? Using props rather than stating the obvious is a good way to avoid that pitfall. Shredded tissues in someone's hand, an open scrapbook on a bedside table, mascara smears under eyes, too many empty wine bottles in a recycling bin—all of these are props that show sadness without the writer having to hit the reader over the head.

How much better to see that character's sadness than to be told he's sad without anything to convince us. These props or suggestions can work in conjunction with something obvious. For example, a character might tell a friend she is sad and then you, the writer, can use many details to suggest that sadness, backing up her statement.

Or the suggestion can give us insights into a character's emotion. Suppose a character wants to hide her sadness from her mother. You can have her state quite blatantly that she's fine, even happy. But everything around her suggests the exact opposite. Description and setting show the reader that in fact the character has done nothing but cry all day. Here is where concrete detail becomes even more important.

Remember my character Libby in her acting class? She wants to hide her jealousy from someone—herself. Those concrete details helped to build the case for the opposite emotion; instead of the sympathy she said she felt, the reader understood her true emotions. I like how this demonstrates that in conveying emotions, as in many facets of good writing, all of the "rules" are interdependent.

Certainly you will sometimes rely on that perfect image or a strong concrete detail or suggestion as a way to show an emotion effectively. Some scenes need one broad stroke to paint that emotional picture. But there are many times when you need to combine a lot of the elements, as in the scene with Libby and her acting class, to drive home your emotional point most effectively.

Point of View

Point of view is a terrific way to render emotion. A character who sees only the tragic stories in the daily paper, for example, or who lies in bed all day watching home shopping channels and crying is clearly conveying sadness. Looking at the world through a character's eyes shapes the reader's perceptions, illustrating the character's emotional self.

One of the most effective uses of point of view to show emotion is through dialogue. The narrative voice can give us emotional readings with great authority, especially when it is backed by strong language, concrete details, and good props that suggest the emotion.

But using dialogue to show emotion helps us to build characters. I'm sure I don't have to remind you that nothing can undermine your story more than weak dialogue. If it's flat or melodramatic or simply sounds false, you will not be able to be emotionally convincing. However, when well written, dialogue can be one of the most authentic ways to show a character's feelings. You give the character a chance to say what she feels in her own voice.

Conversely, dialogue can be a good way to show what a character feels by what he doesn't say. A strong student paper I read showed a couple on the brink of divorce talking about a chipped plate from their wedding china. Feelings are not discussed, yet the scene is emotionally wrought with them—and tension. Had one of them screamed, "I hate you and I want a divorce!" we certainly would have understood the emotions. But *not* saying what they felt made those emotions seem even stronger.

Point of view can also be shaped by interior monologue, which is another excellent way to show a character's emotions. Let's go back to that scene from my novel *Places to Stay the Night* when Libby is in her acting class.

> Acting class made her feel very self-conscious. They had to do things that seemed irrelevant. Like breathe in a particular way that reminded her of her childbirth classes. Then Carl made them say "Ha." Then, "Ha ha." He kept making them add *Has* until they were laughing like crazy people. To Libby, it didn't make any sense. Heather and Ashley really got into it, laughing

like mad. Libby watched them. Were they really laughing? Or were they acting? Was that the point?

Libby's interior questioning demonstrates her own feelings of inadequacy, her jealousy of Heather and Ashley, her emotional state. In dialogue she would not have revealed this; she's trying too hard to seem happy and confident to everyone. In this interior monologue, we get a pure emotional reading.

The Unpredictable

Indirect action—furiously chopping wood or calling psychics on a 900 number—also can evoke emotion. Don't fall into the trap of stating the emotion you want the reader to see, then forcing your character to act in a predictable emotional way. I've already discussed the dangers of stating an emotion outright without backing it up, but you must carefully choose how you back it up. Like indirect dialogue, indirect action allows the reader to piece together the character's emotional puzzle and keeps the writer from stating the obvious.

This is another overlap of the fictional elements at work in rendering emotion. You can fall into a big cliché trap by stating an emotion and then using an easy or predictable action to illustrate it. For example, stating someone is sad and then showing the person crying can come across as emotionally facile or false rather than reinforcing. Although there is no denying that sadness often results in the action of crying, not all sadness leads there. Can you push the emotional envelope further? Can you take the emotion, the character, and ultimately the reader someplace new?

Not only should you work hard to avoid the predictable, the obvious, and the cliché, but you should even try to subvert the obvious as a way of showing emotion. The obvious response to grief is crying. But what if you had a character respond by laughing? Or making love? I'm not the only person I know who never misses a showing of the *Mary Tyler Moore* episode in which Chuckles the Clown dies and no one can stop laughing.

Let's return again to Libby in her acting class. Her jealousy and unhappiness have been demonstrated in many ways so far: point of view, interior monologue, concrete detail, suggestion. Now look at how the unpredictable brings her to a new emotional place, where she can no longer fool herself about what she feels. Carl, the acting teacher, asks each class member to make a sound that describes his or her center. Libby is worried about being embarrassed. She tries to think of quiet sounds—a sigh or hiccup. But this is what happens.

> And then it was Libby's turn. She hadn't found her center. She was sweaty, panicked. Maybe she had no center. Maybe she was completely hollow, not even a housewife, certainly not a star. The very air in the room seemed to be waiting for her sound. She felt as if someone had ripped out her voice box. Nothing would come out.
>
> From beside her George farted.
>
> "Good!" Carl said.
>
> Heather and Ashley giggled.
>
> "Wait!" Libby shouted.
>
> But they were already on to the next exercise. Carl was talking in that slow hypnotic voice. Everyone thought she had farted publicly, that her center was that low and ridiculous. Libby wanted more than anything, in that moment, to be back home.

The scene takes an unpredictable, even comic, turn that leads the reader—and Libby—to an honest emotional place. Libby has a longing for home, a place where she was loved and appreciated, where her center was something substantial.

Indirect action, irony, humor—they all take the reader somewhere fresh and unexpected. They leave cliché behind. Using them forces the writer to look at emotions and the character in a different light.

Emotional Complexity

Perhaps the most important thing to remember when searching for emotional honesty is that emotion is not one-dimensional. Emotions are complex and often mixed together. I once had a student who described a woman who was unhappy in her marriage this way: "Chloe was angry. She was also sad and confused. She was disappointed. She felt anxious and afraid." Although the writer did not successfully convey what was at the emotional heart of Chloe, she did stumble upon an important truth in writing emotions: They are complicated and often a mix of many different emotions.

Think of a bride on her wedding day. It would be too easy and too flat to describe her as simply happy. Instead, she is excited, apprehensive, worried, fearful, anxious, joyful, smug—so many emotions! But if you, the writer, can capture her feelings exactly right—with the perfect turn of a phrase, or simile, or fresh image—you will tell the reader more about this character and this story than you can imagine.

One of the things we need to do when rendering emotions is to see our characters as complex beings who experience a range of feelings. If we start a story with a character in despair, we have to move that character through many emotions before our story ends with him hopeful. Also, the faces of despair and hope and every emotion are multifaceted. Just as sadness is not just crying, each emotion is not represented by one dimension. The layers of an emotion often hold other emotions too.

Think again of Libby. She isn't simply jealous of Heather and Ashley; she is disappointed, confused, frightened, worried. She moves through that to longing for home, which also holds layers of other feelings. But for Libby to jump off the page, her emotions have to be rich and complex, to inform the reader of new ideas and authentic feelings. There are times when an emotion is simply rendered. There are even times when the emotion itself is simple. But in evoking character, remember that emotions shape and color your character and demand complexity.

RED LANTERNS

Ayn Rand wrote in *Atlas Shrugged*: "He liked to observe emotions; they were like red lanterns strung along the dark unknown of another's personality, marking vulnerable points." In the pages that follow, there are explorations of the different emotions writers use most; there are examples of where writers go wrong in trying to render those emotions; there are examples from literature that demonstrate how other writers have written emotions well; there are exercises that will help you to capture emotions. I hope these pages will be your red lanterns, leading the way to a deeper understanding of how characters feel and how writers can put those feelings into words.

PART TWO
THE EMOTIONS

ANGER

"Outrage, combining as it does shock, anger, reproach, and helplessness, is perhaps the most unmanageable, the most demoralizing of all the emotions." This quote from Margery Allingham's *Death of a Ghost* captures much about anger. True, Allingham is describing outrage here; but anger has so many gradations, so many levels, it is indeed—for the writer at least—one of the most unmanageable emotions.

Look up *anger* in your thesaurus, and the synonyms for it practically tumble off the page: *wrath, ire, madness, infuriation, enragement, soreness; exasperate, nettle, pique, vex, irritate, incense, ruffle, roil*. However, we tend to write anger as a flat or simple emotion, something closer to rage. We too often show an angry character scream or put a fist through a wall or beat up a neighbor. These actions show one level of anger, but what makes the emotion so interesting—and challenging—is that it has many different faces.

My favorite way to think about anger is with cooking analogies. Some anger simmers, some boils, some boils over, some bakes, some is mixed thoroughly with other emotions. Sometimes anger leaves you feeling fried or shaken or tossed about. Sometimes anger leaves you sated.

The important thing to remember is that anger doesn't have to be so difficult to convey. All of those synonyms represent some form of anger. Is your character simply piqued? Or is she enraged? Someone who is piqued might merely roll her eyes or shake her head. An enraged character is more likely to pound a brick wall with his fists. Two angry characters, two degrees of anger, two very different ways of expressing the emotion.

Yesterday, thinking about anger, I took note of how often and to what degree I experienced the emotion. When my three-year-old dilly-dallied in the yard while I tried to get him in the car and to school on time, I got angry. How did I show that kind of anger? I muttered, "Come on, come on, come on already!" When I got a ticket for parking in what I thought was a legal space, I got angry. I ran after the meter maid, yelling about injustice. When my baby-sitter showed up fifteen minutes late and almost caused me to miss a bus I needed to catch, I got angry and was sarcastic and flip with him. When I got off the bus and had to wait almost half an hour for my husband, I was angry. How did I show him? The silent treatment.

Perhaps that sounds like a lot of time spent angry. But we could say that the only time I felt anything close to the stereotypical anger we tend to overdemonstrate was with the meter maid. I was frustrated, annoyed, irritated—all different forms of anger. Don't rely on the obvious with this one, and you will find it a manageable emotion to convey after all.

BAD EXAMPLES

George was mad as a hornet (mad as a wet hen, mad as hell).

Clichés always make us stop and ask questions like, "How mad is a hornet?" They have stopped working from overuse. None of the above tells us how or why George is mad; none of them tells us what his anger is like.

"You're an idiot!" Joseph yelled.
"Go to hell!" Robin yelled back.
"I hate you!" Joseph yelled at Robin as he got into his car.
"I hate you!" Robin yelled.

We definitely have two angry people here, but the writer hasn't worked very hard to make that anger alive. Instead, she has relied on the verb "yell" and too many exclamation marks. Such exclamatory dialogue flattens the emotion rather than intensifies it.

Peter punches him hard in the stomach. Frank jabs at Peter anyway, once, twice, three times in the gut before Peter manages to land a fist squarely on Frank's jaw. Frank reels backwards, then crashes into the bar, sending bottles and people scurrying.

This reads more like a scene description from a Van Damme movie than an effort to show either Peter's or Frank's anger. It is all action without any emotion.

GOOD EXAMPLES

One way to convey an emotion is to use another emotion to express it. For example, in Stanley Elkin's story "A Poetics for Bullies," the narrator opens by telling us whom he hates. Certainly this paragraph could also be an example for hate. But the voice is so angry that his hatred is really stemming from anger.

> I'm Push the bully, and what I hate are new kids and sissies, dumb kids and smart, rich kids, poor kids, kids who wear glasses, talk funny, show off, patrol boys and wise guys and kids who pass pencils and water the plants—and cripples, especially cripples. I love nobody loved.

In one scene of "The Dead," James Joyce has Gabriel's emotions happen in stages. Gabriel moves from anger to lust to jealousy to humiliation to fear and finally to understanding. These stages represent how emotions work to build characters in our fiction. Let's look at how Joyce described that first stage, anger.

> —I am thinking about a person long ago who used to sing that song.
> —And who was the person long ago? asked Gabriel, smiling.
> —It was a person I used to know in Galway when I was living with my grandmother, she said.
> The smile passed away from Gabriel's face. A dull anger began to gather again at the back of his mind and the dull fires of his lust began to glow angrily in his veins.
> —Someone you were in love with? he asked ironically.

E.L. Doctorow shows anger through dialogue in this passage from his story "The Writer in the Family." Unlike our bad example where angry dialogue is simply name-calling and yelling, Doctorow is able to utilize humor, voice and character while conveying emotion.

> My mother slammed down the phone. "He can't even die when he wants to!" she cried. "Even death comes second to Mama! What are they afraid of, the shock will kill her?

Nothing can kill her. She's indestructible! A stake through the heart couldn't kill her!"

EXERCISES

1. Even in the short passage from Joyce's "The Dead," we see Gabriel pass through several emotions on his way to anger. He begins smiling, then feels a dull anger that fuels lust. Try this yourself. Imagine that a character has just given this piece of news to another character: "Actually, this isn't my first pregnancy. I gave a baby away for adoption twenty years ago, when I was in art school." First decide who is receiving the news: her mother? her husband? her best friend? Then write a response from that character's point of view. Be sure the response leads the character through at least three emotions (remember that Gabriel experiences more emotions than what our small example shows). It's all right if anger isn't one of the emotions.

Objective: To write an emotional arc for a character to move through.

2. Write a paragraph in the voice of someone who, like Push the bully, talks about hate but conveys anger. First you must choose two emotions that feed off each other the way hate and anger do. Here are some suggestions: passion and love, fear and shame, loneliness and despair. Be sure the voice owns up to one of the emotions and doesn't mention the other. How convincing is the unmentioned one?

Objective: To explore the use of voice in conveying emotion.

3. Look in your own thesaurus for all the words synonymous with anger. Then make a line, using ten degrees of anger. Choose any ten synonyms. You might start with pique and end with outrage. Be sure to move from mildest to strongest. You might choose all degrees of mild anger or all degrees of explosive anger. The important thing is to build from the first one to the tenth.

Objective: To examine the finer points of this emotion. It would be a good idea to try this exercise with other emotions too. Try it with hate and contentment.

ANXIETY

Sitting here at my computer writing about anxiety reminds me of all the things I am anxious about. There is the obvious worry: Will I be able to successfully explain how to depict anxiety in a character? But then there are other ones bubbling to the surface. In the next week I have to decide whether or not to have amniocentesis, and I have anxiety about the decision, about the test itself, about the results. Then, too, I am anxious because I've had such bad morning sickness that I'm behind on my writing deadlines, late in reading my students' papers. I am even anxious over the fact that we are having guests for dinner tonight and I have nothing planned or prepared.

As you can see by my own list of worries, anxiety comes from matters large and small. Anxiety is worrying to an extreme. I think of the Dorothy Parker short story "A Telephone Call." A woman is waiting for a man to call her. The longer she waits, the more anxious she becomes. She has the operator call her to be sure the phone is working, she paces, she shouts at the telephone, she plays mind games with herself. With each sentence Parker raises the anxiety level until it is nearly tangible. All that worrying over a simple phone call!

In that one story, Parker employs several methods to depict anxiety: interior monologue, physical reactions, obsessive behavior, and having the character focus her anxiety on one concern (the telephone call that doesn't come). When I told you everything I was anxious about, you probably didn't feel my anxiety the way you would want your readers to feel a character's anxiety. They were too diffused; I didn't linger on one or emphasize how my anxiety manifested itself.

Anaïs Nin wrote that anxiety "makes others feel as you might when a drowning man holds on to you. You want to save him, but you know he will strangle you with his panic." That is the question to ask yourself when you want to see if you've successfully portrayed anxiety: Are you strangling the reader with his panic?

BAD EXAMPLES

>   Gloria waited anxiously.

By using the adverb *anxiously*, the writer here actually diluted Gloria's anxiety. How much better this example would be if we saw *how* Gloria waited anxiously. Does she talk to herself? Suck on the ends of her hair? The opportunity exists to bring both Gloria and her anxiety into sharper focus, but the adverb gets in the way. This writer certainly doesn't let Gloria's panic strangle us.

>   June wondered if the kids were all right. She wondered if they had anything to drink at the party. She was worried that something had happened to them.

This writer fell into the bad habit of telling us about June's anxiety rather than showing us. If June had used interior monologue we would not only hear her anxiety come to life, we would also get insight into her character.

>   Would that doctor ever come out? Jon wondered. He bit his nails and tapped his foot nervously.

Nail biting, foot tapping, fingers drumming, sweaty palms, butterflies in the stomach, a trickle of sweat, and pacing are all tired ways to show anxiety.

GOOD EXAMPLES

Look at how Thom Jones portrays the anxiety of a woman who realizes she is dying in his short story "I Want to Live!" Notice how effectively interior monologue is used.

>   But those people in the hospital rooms, gray and dying, that was her. Could such a thing be possible? To die? Really? Yes, at some point she guessed you did die. But her? Now? So soon? With so little time to get used to the idea?

A second effective way to depict anxiety is through obsessive behavior. Jane Shapiro does this in her short story "Poltergeists" by having the narrator, who's waiting for her teenage son to come home, count off time in intervals. The intervals grow shorter as her anxiety increases.

At two, Zack's expected arrival time, he wasn't home. I decided to read. At two-thirty, he wasn't home. At three, he wasn't home. At three-fifteen, the phone rang once, then stopped. At three-thirty, I heard Bibi's car slowly approaching, coasting in—she was driving with admirable care, and they were almost home. But they weren't. The car paused, then moved on. When I went to look out, it was gone. Empty street, in quiet darkness.

A third effective way to show anxiety is through physical reactions, as Joyce Carol Oates does in her short story "Where Are You Going, Where Have You Been?" Connie, a teenager coming into her own sexuality, has gone for a joyride with two "boys." Then she realizes they are grown men and that she may be in danger.

Ellie turned for the first time and Connie saw with shock that he wasn't a kid either—he had a fair, hairless face, cheeks reddened slightly as if the veins grew too close to the surface of his skin, the face of a forty-year-old baby. Connie felt a wave of dizziness rise in her at this sight and she stared at him as if waiting for something to change the shock of the moment, make it all right again.

EXERCISES

1. Write a one-page scene entirely in interior monologue in which the narrator is anxious about getting some news, such as test results from a doctor, a job offer, a home pregnancy test.

Objective: To use interior monologue to depict anxiety as well as to reveal insight into the narrator's character.

2. Without using dialogue, write a one- or two-page scene in which a character is in danger. Use description and action to evoke the danger and the character's anxiety about it.

Objective: To use physical reactions to show anxiety.

3. Choose a seemingly minor reason to produce anxiety, such as an invitation to a party, running out of hot water, a rainy day, and write a one-page scene in which a character obsesses on that concern. Be sure the character's anxiety level rises as the scene progresses.

Objective: To tap into the heart of anxiety. Even a small thing can cause great panic.

APATHY

I suppose the most well-known expression of apathy is Rhett Butler's comment to Scarlett O'Hara in *Gone With the Wind*: "My dear, I don't give a damn." Although that sentence appears in Margaret Mitchell's 1936 novel, it's the dashing Clark Gable whom most of us imagine when we hear those words. Perhaps literature's best contribution to apathy is Bartleby in Herman Melville's "Bartleby the Scrivener," who responds to every request with an indifferent "I would prefer not to."

What exactly is apathy? It is a lack of emotion or interest or feeling. It is indifference. To me, apathy is one of the hardest emotions to express well; it is basically a nonemotion, a numbing or even deadening, an erasure of feeling. Think of Bartleby in his dull, dead-end job. Or Rhett Butler at the end of his love and tolerance for Scarlett O'Hara.

But to write an apathetic character well, writers risk many missteps. The character might come across as hard or cruel instead of devoid of feeling. An apathetic person could act cruelly, or his indifference could manifest itself in a way that seems hard. But apathy is a more flat, more linear emotion than cruelty.

Another problem that could arise in trying to draw an apathetic character is that she might seem unlikable. Perhaps that is your intention. But if it isn't, you risk losing your reader's attention or sympathy because the apathetic character is simply too awful to want to read about.

Perhaps the worst misstep is to mistake apathy for boredom. We meet a character whose responses are dull, who lacks interior reflection, a character who is flat. One of the biggest sins of writing is to bore your reader—with language, with plot, and with character. An apathetic character is not boring. He might be baffling, frustrating, pitiful, or pathological but never boring.

Finally, apathy should be used for a reason. Like all other emotions, it needs to move the character and the reader somewhere. It isn't good enough to depict a bad husband as apathetic; his apathy must have a point. Even this most *non*emotion must work emotionally.

BAD EXAMPLES

> John went to his boring job every day, Monday through Friday, from 9 to 5. He punched the time clock. He worked. He ate lunch at noon, a bologna sandwich on white bread. He got home by 5:30 where his wife was waiting with a meatloaf dinner.

The above example is boring. We don't see John as apathetic; we see him and his life and even his wife as boring. His boredom's lack of motivation, which could make it more interesting and more understandable, makes it just the opposite.

> "Help me," Donna begged. "I think my leg is broken."
> Her husband loomed above her, the point of one ski pressing into the soft down of her jacket. He hesitated, as if surveying the damage.
> "No," he said finally, and schussed away, leaving a fine spray of wet snow on Donna's face and hair.

Donna's husband is not apathetic here; he's cruel. But because he acts unfeeling, this writer thought she was showing apathy.

> Jessica had been in her room, mostly in her bed, since she'd graduated two months ago. Despite her parents' bribes and begging, she chose to stay there, throwing Cheet-o's bags on the floor, neglecting her fish, and counting her split ends.

Jessica is certainly apathetic, so this story could be effective. But what if the writer never explores *why* she's staying in bed or never gets her out of bed? Then she hasn't used apathy as part of an emotional spectrum. The story would end exactly where it begins: Jessica is apathetic. The reader would leave it without understanding Jessica or apathy.

GOOD EXAMPLES

In his short story "Orientation" Daniel Orozco succeeds where the writer in the first bad example fails. Orozco manages to capture the apathy of office life by taking the reader on a tour of one and revealing in a matter-of-fact, unfeeling way the workers' secrets. With terrific irony, the secrets get more and more bizarre, but the narrator's tone never changes; it remains indifferent, apathetic, as the reader grows more horrified.

> Kevin Howard sits in that cubicle over there. He is a serial killer, the one they call the Carpet Cutter, responsible for the mutilations across town. We're not supposed to know that, so don't let on.

Slawomii Mirozek manages to use apathy in the way the writer of the second bad example failed. Mirozek's "The Elephant" shows a man whose indifference does cause cruelty, but he is not purposefully cruel. Rather, he is apathetic about something—his job—and we understand the reason for his apathy (and therefore we understood the consequences of it).

> The director of the Zoological Gardens had shown himself to be an upstart. He regarded his animals simply as stepping stones on the road of his own career. He was indifferent to the educational importance of his establishment. In his zoo the giraffe had a short neck, the badger had no burrow, and the whistlers, having lost all interest, whistled rarely and with some reluctance.

Finally, look at how Walter Kirn uses apathy as part of an emotional spectrum in his story "Thumbsucker." At the start of the story, Kirn describes a thirteen-year-old boy's pleasure in sucking his thumb.

> The effect when the thumb touched my lips was subtle and encompassing. Because I sometimes watched myself in a mirror, doubling my sense of self-communion, I know how I looked at the moment of closure. Above my greedily flexing cheeks, my eyes would soften and blur as though I'd just put drops in. My forehead would relax and lose its lines. From the rhythmic bullfrog swelling of my throat, it appeared I was actually taking nourishment. I was.

Kirn uses apathy as the final rung on an emotional ladder instead of as a simple, flat characteristic. By so thoroughly describing pleasure, he can show the reader its emotional opposite—apathy—in a believable and moving way.

> For the last time, I sought solace in my thumb. I felt nothing, nothing came out—no comfort, no relief. My thumb felt dead and so did my body.

EXERCISES

1. We often think of apathy in terms of social or political events. In an election year we hear a lot about apathetic voters. Or there is a generalization that Big Business or government offices are apathetic. In the way that Orozco used the setting of an office and irony to show apathy, write a two-page tour of one of the following:

- IBM headquarters
- a college dorm on election day
- an IRS audit
- a city hospital's emergency room

Objective: To use apathy to evoke feeling from your reader.

2. Create a character in a one-page sketch who, like Mirozek's director of the Zoological Gardens, is indifferent to his surroundings because of his personal agenda. What type of need or ambition would a character have that would cause him to be apathetic to the plight of others?

Objective: To find a motivation that would lead to apathy and therefore make the apathy believable.

3. In Maurice Sendak's children's story *Pierre*, the title character is an apathetic little boy who shouts, "I don't care!" even when he is faced with being eaten by a lion. Write a one-page fairy tale that stars an apathetic character. Give your character a fanciful name and put that person in fantastic situations. Have fun with this one! Your character, like Pierre, should respond with, "I don't care!" But you decide if there will be a final event that will move the character away from apathy.

Objective: To use fancy and humor in your writing.

CONFUSION

The trickiest part about conveying confusion is to convey it clearly, without confusing the reader. By definition, confusion is disorder or bewilderment. Your character is flustered and befuddled, but it is important that she doesn't leave the reader flustered and befuddled.

The confused character is trying to assemble either stimuli or information without any sense or order; the reader, on the other hand, needs to recognize the character's confusion, not join in it. The character might mistake something—an emotion, a scene, a reaction—for something else; the reader needs to see that confusion rather than make the same mistake.

The other pitfall in depicting confusion is overloading the character with physical responses (head swims, palms sweat) or with too many stimuli (doorbells ring, a baby cries, a shirt scented with unfamiliar perfume is found—all simultaneously). Confusion is often an overload, but more realistically it's a befuddlement: If he loves me why is he walking out that door?

It's easy to simply place our character in chaos, draw a confusing scene, and pronounce the character confused. What's more difficult is to understand the emotional source of the confusion and then to depict it convincingly. When a man I loved told me he loved me but needed time apart, my head didn't swim. My confusion kept me awake at night reading old love letters, searching for clues. When my three-year-old doesn't understand why he made me angry, his confusion often makes him act even worse.

In *Fiction, Oddly Enough* Mary Virginia Micka offers this insight into the true nature of confusion: "It is while trying to get everything straight in my head that I get confused." Real confusion usually doesn't manifest itself in erratic action. It remains internal. For this reason, it can be difficult to evoke accurately on the page.

BAD EXAMPLES

> Gilda's head was swimming with confusion. She thought she might faint, right there in front of everyone. Or worse, throw up.

> Elly watched Joe as he calmly threw his clothes into a suitcase. After ten years together, how could he just walk out like this? The telephone started to ring and she heard the boys come in from outside, calling for something to drink, to eat, to do. Now the cat was wrapping its tail around her legs, hungry too. Slowly, Elly sank to the floor, holding her head, as if that could help her figure any of this out.

> The letter made everything worse. How had Mark mailed it from Wyoming when he was supposed to be in Connecticut? And what did he mean with all his talk about blood tests and positive proof at last? And who the hell was this Rebecca?

All of the above examples certainly do show confusion. But they all rely on external factors to depict it and therefore avoid really exploring and honestly depicting the emotion. In the first, we get only physical responses. In the second, we get stimulus overload. And in the third, we simply get information that confuses us too.

GOOD EXAMPLES

Often, with a wonderfully written story, every sentence builds upon every other sentence to ultimately convey one emotion. That can be said of Tillie Olsen's story "I Stand Here Ironing," in which a mother reflects on her nineteen-year-old daughter and her relationship to her. She remembers, sifts, and weighs different times in the girl's life, trying to get everything straight. Here is one example that shows confusion on two levels—the daughter's and the mother's.

> There was a boy she loved painfully through two school semesters. Months later she told me how she had taken pennies from my purse to buy him candy. "Licorice was his favorite and I brought him some every day, but he still liked Jennifer better'n me. Why Mommy?" The kind of question for which there is no answer.

For much of Susan Taylor Chehak's novel *Smithereens*, the young narrator is trying to figure out Frankie, a teenager whom her family sponsored since girlhood and who has now shown up on their door-step. Chehak weighs impressions and information to show us confusion. First, the narrator imagines what her mother thinks of Frankie. Then she contrasts that with what she herself has seen.

> I knew what she was thinking. That she was making up a picture of Frankie's life, imagining a little girl growing up without enough to eat in a cramped and dilapidated shack with a dust floor and no electricity and an outhouse in the back. She was seeing all the pitiful images of neglected and forgotten children that they'd shown in the commercials that the Federation put on TV.
>
> But people like that didn't drive Lincoln Continentals, did they? Or have boxes of gold and silver jewelry with diamonds that looked like maybe they might be real?

Sometimes we search for a way out of our confusion. This is a good contrast to set up to convey that emotion: Show the character confused and trying to figure out a solution. Alice Munro does this in her short story "The Jack Randa Hotel," in which a woman leaves behind her life in Canada to follow an old lover to Australia.

> It is Will's own writing on the envelope. Not a letter to Will, then, but a letter from him. A letter he had sent to Ms. Catherine Thornaby, 491 Hawtre Street. Also in Brisbane. Another hand has scrawled across it "Return to Sender, Died Sept. 13." For a moment, in her disordered state of mind, Gail thinks that this means that Will has died.
>
> She has got to calm down, collect herself, stay out of the sun for a bit.

EXERCISES

1. Reread the final line in the Tillie Olsen example. Then make a list of ten questions "for which there is no answer" that show confusion. Be sure the character being addressed is asked "why." Having a specific listener will help keep you focused.

Objective: To practice using character and voice to express emotion; also, to use other writers' techniques as models in your own work.

2. Susan Taylor Chehak shows confusion by playing with fantasy vs. reality. The narrator's mother imagines one kind of life for Frankie and

the narrator contrasts that with reality. Choose one of the lives below:

- a young woman who claims to be a movie star's mistress
- a homeless man holding a sign that says "Vietnam Vet Needs Your Help"
- the father of triplets
- a mechanic specializing in foreign cars
- a man confessing to be a sought-after serial killer
- Anastasia Romanov, daughter of Nicholas and Alexandra, who was believed to be killed with the rest of her family
- Ringo Starr

Now write a scene describing how that life might be. Then write two questions, like Chehak did, that contrast reality with the imagined life. Use the example from her novel *Smithereens* as a model. Once you've done one, try two more.

Objective: To practice writing confusion clearly and using it as a process for figuring something out.

3. Alice Munro has her character come up with simple solutions to sort through disorder: calm down, get out of the sun. Make a list of twenty other simple solutions. Choose two of them for each of the situations below. Which ones work as a way to sort through disorder and confusion? Why?

- That can't be Alexander. He's supposed to be dead!
- Elise is positive this is the way back home. But she keeps going down dead ends.
- The driving instructor was waiting, but Amanda couldn't remember how to do it.
- The young man at the door was claiming to be her son. But how had he found her after all these years?
- Surely John knows the answer. Everyone stared at him, waiting. Especially the professor.

Objective: To rely on internal thoughts rather than just external events to show confusion.

CONTENTMENT

"O world," Edna St. Vincent Millay wrote in her poem "God's World," "I cannot hold thee close enough!"

Now that is contentment. Closer to satisfaction with the way things are than to happiness, contentment is having what you want. It might be momentary and fleeting, it might have happened long ago, it might be a state of mind. But it is always total satisfaction.

Most of my moments of contentment come at night, just before sleep. On my wedding night, listening to my new husband breathe beside me, I was enveloped by a feeling of completeness, of rightness. One night a few months after my son was born, I woke up and that same feeling came over me: Everything is right with my world.

To render this emotion in fiction we can have a character look at the past, the present, or the future and feel a large sense of satisfaction. Although we might associate that variety of emotion with old age, I think there are people, and more importantly, fictional characters, who live a good part of their lives that way. In fiction, the content character might be the perfect one to bring tragedy or surprise to. Or contentment might be the end of an emotional arc for a character; the writer takes the reader from unhappiness through a series of events to contentment, to the point where the world is so wonderful, the character cannot hold it close enough. However you decide to use this emotion, be aware that you must use it convincingly. You must, in a sense, earn it. A reader is inclined to accept conflict, even tragedy, rather than accept that all is right in the world.

BAD EXAMPLES

. . . And they lived happily ever after.

Okay, maybe it does work at the end of fairy tales, but in fiction you must be wary of pat, easy endings that gloss over the heart of the emotion. We have all read too many stories in which the writer has the characters reach an inauthentic contentment. As readers, we remain unconvinced by such endings. We feel cheated and betrayed by the author, to whom we have given our trust. The author also has betrayed the characters by oversimplifying the conflicts and complexities that lead to the ending. Perhaps your character(s) will live happily ever after, but you have to convince us of that.

> Life was perfect for Nancy. She had two beautiful, well-behaved children and a lovely home with a pool and English garden. Her husband was handsome and kind and they got along well.

As soon as you set up a superlative for a character ("Life was perfect for Nancy"), you set up doubt in the reader's mind. Even the examples that follow seem weak when we're seeking perfection. Don't tell us that something is perfect; show us Nancy's contentment in how she acts, looks, speaks. If we see how Nancy's feelings are manifest, we'll be more likely to believe them.

> Terry had to pinch herself to be sure she was awake.

This is a screaming cliché! It doesn't indicate contentment. It just tries to push the reader's familiarity quotient: If she's pinching herself she must be really pleased. As with all clichés, the writer is either being lazy, taking a shorthand approach, or not exploring the particulars of the character or situation deeply enough. Should we take the statement literally (Terry is unsure if she is conscious)? Or should we take it figuratively (Terry is so content she cannot believe it)? With clichés like this one, the reader most often feels nothing. We move past with no clear sense of what emotion the character is feeling.

GOOD EXAMPLES

Amy Bloom gives us the contentment found in looking back at one's childhood in her story "Love Is Not a Pie." The strength of this example is in the details as she chronicles the perfect days a family spent at a cabin every summer. We feel the contentment of the characters through the selection of these details and because of their specificity. We believe the narrator's contentment because we, too, experience it. We hear the birds "screaming and trilling," taste the cake and cold spaghetti, take part in the comforting routine. Below is a sampling from the morning routine, but the story spends glorious time recalling each part of the whole day.

> We had the kind of summer cabin routine that stays with you forever as a model of leisure, of life being enjoyed. We'd get up early, listening to the birds screaming and trilling, and make ourselves some breakfast: cold cereal or toast if the parents were up, cake or cold spaghetti or marshmallows if they were still asleep. Then the parents would get up, my mother first, usually. She'd make a cup of coffee and brush and braid our hair and set us loose. If we were going exploring, she'd put three sandwiches and three pieces of fruit in a bag, with an army blanket. Otherwise, she'd just wave to us headed down to the lake. We'd come back at lunchtime. . . . It was the most beautiful time.

Cathleen Schine gives us a character in her novel *The Love Letter* who is completely content with herself. In fiction, this is a perfect character to undergo some kind of turmoil, something that will force her to look at her life anew. Notice how Schine, by repeating forms of the word *dissatisfy*, creates a tone that suggests this character soon will not feel so contented.

> She drove beneath overhanging branches and new summery leaves, and she was not only content, but pleased by her own contentment, as if happiness were an accomplishment, a good grade, an honor. She had never liked being dissatisfied. She found it so dissatisfying.

In this excerpt from Edna O'Brien's short story "The Doll," she uses the phrase "untoward happiness." Not only does that phrase describe contentment, but the first paragraph of the story, in which the narrator tells us about the arrival of a doll for Christmas, captures the emotion through setting—shortly before Christmas—and the use of action to create that setting.

> We made potato stuffing, we made mince pies, we made bowls of trifle, we decorated the windowsills with holly and with tinsel, and it was as if untoward happiness was about to befall us.

EXERCISES

1. Take a moment to really conjure a time in your life when you were content. Perhaps it was in your childhood or when you were in college or newly married. How old were you? Where were you? Who was with you? What about this time in your life made you so content? When you have brought this memory to the forefront of your mind, describe it in specific details. Be sure to take the reader to that time and place with you. Tell it in first person.

Objective: To dig deep into yourself to find how contentment really feels to you.

2. Take the memory you wrote about in the first exercise and turn it into fiction. Change the significant details. If your memory was in summer, make the setting winter. Use a different year, different names for the characters. Write the story in third person. Do not change the emotion or how it felt to experience that emotion.

Objective: To use the memory of a real emotion in a piece of fiction.

3. Like Bloom, O'Brien uses concrete details to convey contentment. They both rely on settings too—summers gone by and Christmas. Choose one of the following settings and, using concrete details, write a paragraph that combines the setting and the details to evoke contentment:

- a honeymoon
- a snowy day
- first grade
- a homecoming

Objective: To practice finding and using concrete details.

CURIOSITY

When we think of curiosity, we think of cats and Pandora first. Since curiosity killed the cat, and we know the kind of trouble Pandora's curiosity got her into, I suggest there are other ways to look at it. Curiosity is not always a negative emotion, despite the connotations we get from it. In fact, it's a desire to know something or to learn something new or unusual.

Somehow though, the rather commendable desire for knowledge leads us other places. From curious we can easily land at nosy or snoopy or even intrusive. A busybody is curious. A gossip with an unwarranted interest in someone's business is considered curious. Someone who pries, who asks too many questions, whose motives for the questions are less than worthy, can, I suppose be, considered curious.

But for me, those traits are closer to other emotions. They are curiosity gone bad. I prefer to think of curiosity more as my son's daily litany of why. He asks why the sun is still up, why his grandparents are old, why we don't eat pasta every night, why he has to turn four when he likes being three so much, and hundreds of other such questions.

A good place to start thinking about how to evoke this emotion is to think of a child. Of course, curiosity is not limited to children. But keeping a child's curiosity in mind is a good way to keep the true emotion in focus. Of course those other adjectives—snoopy, nosy, intrusive—are offshoots of curiosity, but I think it's important to see it as what it really is: the arousal of interest by something novel and extraordinary.

In her book *With a Daughter's Eye*, Mary Catherine Bateson gives this definition of curiosity: "Worlds can be found by a child and an adult bending down and looking together under the grass stems or at the skittering crabs in a tidal pool." That is what you are trying to capture when you try to evoke curiosity in a character.

BAD EXAMPLES

> "Why are the leaves turning color?"
>
> "It's autumn."
>
> "Why?"
>
> "Because summer is over."
>
> The little girl seemed satisfied. Then she asked, "Why is summer over?"

Certainly this shows curiosity. But it's too cute, too facile. The writer could use the emotion better by giving the reader some insight either into the characters or into the reason for the child's questions.

> Mrs. Perkins peeked out the window, careful to keep her face hidden by partially closed venetian blinds. There was that young Mrs. Burns, all tarted up, getting in her fancy car and going . . . where? Mrs. Perkins wondered. Where does a person go dressed like that in the middle of the day? Slowly she moved away from the window and shuffled over to the phone. "Hello? Edna?" she said, in a whisper. "You know Mrs. Burns next door to me?"

This is a delightful portrayal of a busybody, the neighbor who can't mind her own business. It can be argued that this shows curiosity; perhaps it does. But the writer has twisted that emotion into something else—nosiness, intrusiveness, even betrayal.

> Simon wondered what Elisabeth's breast would feel like. Soft, he supposed. Satisfied, he closed his eyes and went to sleep.

This writer was onto something, but he left it too soon to fully develop the wonderful curiosity that comes with sex and/or adolescence. Curiosity is larger than just one question that is so simply answered.

GOOD EXAMPLES

Barbara Kingsolver uses a mother-daughter conversation to show a child's curiosity in her short story "Quality Time." However, she doesn't simply rely on the questions the little girl, Rennie, asks her mother; she gives the child's curiosity and her mother's response to it more depth by allowing her mother to reflect on the reasons for the questions. In fact, the mother thinks of the conversation as "a toboggan ride, threatening at every moment to fly out of control." Miriam, the mother, responds both externally and internally when Rennie asks her what happens when someone dies.

> "I'm not sure, Rennie. I think maybe what happens is that you think back over your life, about all the nice things you've done and the people who've been your friends, and then you close your eyes and . . . it's quiet." She was going to say, ". . . and go to sleep," but she's read that sleep and death shouldn't be equated, that it can cause children to fear bedtime. "What do you think?"

Julia Alvarez uses curiosity in her short story "Snow" as a way to expose larger themes. A young immigrant girl's curiosity about snow, which she has never seen, becomes a metaphor for the themes of alienation and acceptance that are explored in the short story.

> All my life I had heard about the white crystals that fell out of American skies in the winter. From my desk I watched the fine powder dust the sidewalk and parked cars below. Each flake was different, Sister Zoe said, like a person, irreplaceable and beautiful.

Jeffrey Eugenides uses the curiosity of a group of teenaged boys about a family of girls to explore the unknown territories of life and death and sex in his novel *The Virgin Suicides*. In this passage, one of the boys has gained entry into the Lisbon girls' home. The emotion is evoked through the awestruck reverence the voice bestows upon the details of the girls' lives.

> He came back to us with stories of bedrooms filled with crumpled panties, of stuffed animals hugged to death by the passion of the girls, of a crucifix draped with a brassiere, of gauzy chambers of canopied beds, and of the effluvia of so many young girls becoming women together in the same cramped space. In the bathroom, running the faucet to cloak the sounds of his search, Peter Sissen found Mary Lisbon's secret cache of cosmetics tied up in a sock under the sink: tubes of red lipstick and the second skin of blush and base.

EXERCISES

1. Write a one-page conversation between a parent and a child in which the child is curious about something and asking a lot of questions. Be sure the parent gives us insight through her own thoughts into some larger issue. For example, in the Barbara Kingsolver story, the mother is thinking about the death of a relative when the child begins asking her about death.

Objective: To practice using interior monologue juxtaposed with dialogue to show feelings.

2. Choose a large theme such as death, hope, or abandonment. Now choose a metaphor to represent that theme. Remember how Julia Alvarez used snow as a metaphor for alienation and acceptance. Write a scene in which someone's curiosity about the chosen metaphor reveals the larger theme.

Objective: To practice writing in metaphor as a way to explore themes and emotions.

3. Part of curiosity is discovery. The girl in "Snow" learns something from seeing her first snowfall; Rennie's questions in "Quality Time" force the mother to think about death and the future; and Peter Sissen's discoveries in *The Virgin Suicides* help to illuminate some things about a teenaged girl's life. Write a two- or three-page sketch in which a character's curiosity leads to an important discovery. Some ideas might be: a girl curious about her young lover's true feelings looks through his dresser; a young boy curious about sex looks through his older brother's things; a child curious about her biological parents looks through her adoptive parents' safe-deposit box. Or think of one of your own.

Objective: To follow the continuum of an emotion: Curiosity leads to discovery.

DESIRE

Jane Smiley wrote in *Ordinary Love*: "In my experience, there is only one motivation, and that is desire." In *The Song of the Lark*, Willa Cather wrote: "There is only one big thing—desire. And before it, when it is big, all is little." And in the poem "Denouement," Adélia Prado wrote: "Compared to my heart's desire / the sea is a drop." Desire is obviously a weighty emotion.

Even the things we associate with it—my heart's desire, *A Streetcar Named Desire*—are large and meaningful, sexy and dramatic, important. Our dictionaries might tell us that desire is simply a wanting or wish, but we know better. It is a passion for something, a craving.

Often, desire is used to express sexual appetites. In fact, that is the biggest pitfall in trying to convey this emotion. True, it can mean a sexual hunger. But a better way to think of desire is to give it the power of sexuality even if the focus is not sexual. Then you get the feeling of the intensity of this emotion.

As a child, my heart's desire was a Barbie wedding gown. But my mother refused, on principle and economic sensibility, to ever buy me one. Yet my desire never faded; in fact, it grew. So much so that years later, in my adulthood, a friend showed me how she had kept all of her Barbies and their clothes and tiny shoes in their case. She opened the lilac wardrobe and there, amid stewardess uniforms, bathing suits, and Jackie Kennedy outfits, rested the wedding dress, just as I remembered it. And it caused my heart to lurch still, the way passing an old lover on a busy street might. Such is the power of desire.

How do we best capture that power as writers trying to convey desire? I always believe conjuring that desire in yourself will help you to better understand what the emotion feels like, and understanding helps you to express it in your writing. Desire can bring to mind something overly romantic, and you must be cautious not to cheapen or diminish the emotion by using easy images of sexual desire.

BAD EXAMPLES

> "I want you," Elly whispered, and she did want him, with her whole heart and soul.

This is generic brand X desire. Filled with clichés—her whole heart and soul—it doesn't read like a real person with a real desire.

> Paul really wanted that black Cougar with the zebra striped upholstery.
>
> "Too much money," his brother told him. He pointed at a copper-colored Duster. "That's what you can afford."
>
> Paul opened the Duster's door and sat inside. Someone had hung a pine tree shaped air freshener in it and the whole car smelled like Christmas.
>
> "I'll take it," Paul said.

There is some nice writing here ("the whole car smelled like Christmas") but the emotion of desire is absent. Paul says he wants the Cougar, but we never really experience his desire. Plus, he gives it up so easily.

> Molly made a list of everything she wanted:
> Golden curls like Beatrice.
> A doll that wets like Mary-Jane's.
> A green velvet dress like her cousin Marie.
> Freckles like her sister Susan's.
> Now, she thought, how can I get every one of these things?

This simple list does give us good insight into Molly's character. But rather than desire, it reads like jealousy. Desire is a great wish or craving for something, not a need to have what everyone else has.

GOOD EXAMPLES

In her story "The Interview," Ruth Prawer Jhabvala shows us a world in India through the eyes of a narrator who is a young husband from the educated caste. It is his brother's duty to take care of him and his family until he finds suitable work, something that he has been unable to do. At the end of the story, the narrator is full of regret; in the passage that follows, he speaks of desire for his sister-in-law. But in that desire we see a larger desire—for a different kind of life—and a realization of his own unhappiness.

> Then I thought again about my sister-in-law and I thought that if I were kind to her, she would continue to be kind to me. I became quite excited when I thought about being kind to her. I would know then how her big breasts would feel under the blouse, how warm they were and how soft. And I would know about the inside of her mouth with the big strong teeth. . . . I became very excited when I thought of it; but when the excitement had passed, I was sad.

The word *desire* might conjure physical desire or the desires that come with the things we dream of and wish for. When Richard Wright shows us a boy's desire for a gun in the story "Almos' a Man," it is with surprising tenderness, proving that it is the way the emotion is conveyed rather than the object desired that convinces the reader of its authenticity.

> He poured his plate full of molasses and sopped it up slowly with a chunk of cornbread. When his father and brother had left the kitchen, he still sat and looked again at the guns in the catalogue, longing to muster courage enough to present his case to his mother. Lawd, ef Ah only had tha pretty one! He could almost feel the slickness of the weapon with his fingers. If he had a gun like that he would polish it and keep it shining so it would never rust. N Ah'd keep it loaded, by Gawd!

Certainly life and death are thematically well suited to convey desire. But Alison Baker explores how large and ridiculous desire can be in her short story "How I Came West, and Why I Stayed." Often we forget that humor and irony are good vehicles for rendering emotion.

> "All my life," I began, and I prayed my voice wouldn't shake, "there was nothing I wanted more than to be a cheerleader. All through my childhood my parents held up cheerleaders as role models for me. 'My dream,' my dad used to say, 'is that someday you'll be just like them.' We went to every game. And when I watched the professional games on TV—oh, I burned with the desire to be out there with them, leaping and

bending and rolling on national television, and flinging my arms out to embrace the whole world!"

EXERCISES

1. Remember my burning desire for a Barbie wedding dress? What has been an object of your desire? Forget about life's large issues, such as life or death, great wealth or success, and concentrate instead on something concrete you have desired: a cocker spaniel? a lime green VW bug? a big screen TV? Write a page about that object and your desire for it.

Objective: To focus on how the emotion really feels to you and to practice putting that emotion into words.

2. Choose a big issue this time: life, death, a child, wealth, fame, or one of your own. Write a one-page scene describing a character who has this desire. Were you able to express that character's desire as well as you expressed your own in exercise one?

Objective: To use your own emotions to inform your characters.

3. Now choose something humorous as a vehicle for rendering desire. Remember Alison Baker's cheerleaders? The important point is that Baker made that desire believable and real. You should be able to do the same for your characters. Invent a character who desires something humorous or lighthearted rather than serious: to win the Betty Crocker Bake-Off, to be the tallest girl in her class, to learn to play the accordion, to get selected for *The Price Is Right*. Or think of one of your own. Now write a scene in which your character is describing her desire to another character. Remember not to condescend to your character and not to laugh at her. Your character's desire to play the accordion is as real as your desire for a cocker spaniel.

Objective: To create a real, sympathetic character. Remember that you are not your character, but that your emotional insight can—and should—inform your characters.

DESPAIR

It is hard to relive the times of despair we've experienced, even for the sake of our fiction. But if we turn our backs on our own emotions, we cannot have our characters accurately convey—or even feel—those emotions themselves. In fiction, if we hide from emotion we get flat characters.

Perhaps some of us have never felt utter despair, the way a drug addict or a homeless person might. Like all things, despair is relative. But whatever the cause, it still feels the same—an utter loss of hope, a sense of futility or defeat.

There was a time in my life when I was living alone in New York City, broke, trying desperately to write in between working odd jobs at odd hours, and I came down with pneumonia. The cost of a subway token then was seventy-five cents. Sick and shivering, I walked through a cold February rain to the ATM, where it flashed the words at me: Insufficient Funds. I tried to obtain lower and lower amounts, but the response was the same. I had completely run out of money. Walking over thirty blocks to see my doctor that day, wet and cold and sick, I felt what I can only describe as despair.

But despair is such a dark, heavy-handed emotion that to describe it can come across as more maudlin than hopeless, more self-pitying than futile, and you can risk losing sympathy for your character. There are ways to show despair more clearly and to avoid those pitfalls.

For example, compare a happy time with the time of despair to lend balance and perspective to the emotion. Or use a child's viewpoint for a fresh way to show something so dark. Or, as oxymoronic as this might sound, use humor when conveying despair.

BAD EXAMPLES

> There was nowhere to turn. Jim had reached the end of his rope. It was over, all of it.

This writer has managed to fit a lot of clichés into a short space: "nowhere to turn," "end of his rope." They don't really inform the emotion of despair at all.

> Oh, Gail thought, what have I done to deserve this? No one to love me, no one who cares. She wept, alone.

It's maudlin and melodramatic; I can't believe in the authenticity of Gail's despair.

> It was winter, a night so cold and dark that Jake shivered alone by the fireplace long after the fire went out.

This writing is too heavy-handed. Although it is true that the use of external setting to mirror a character's internal landscape can be effective, this writer has gone overboard.

GOOD EXAMPLES

Here is an example of comparing/contrasting despair and contentment, from the opening lines of William March's novel *The Bad Seed*. This approach heightens our awareness of the despair, but tempers and complicates the emotion by comparing it to a different one.

> Later that summer, when Mrs. Penmark looked back and remembered, when she was caught up in despair so deep that she knew there was no way out, no solution whatever for the circumstances that encompassed her, it seemed to her that June seventh, the day of the Fern Grammar School picnic, was the day of her last happiness, for never since then had she known contentment or peace.

Mark Richard's story "The Birds for Christmas" embodies the emotion of despair. By using a child's voice, he manages to make the despair even more painful, more fresh, more evident, and certainly more heartbreaking. In addition, he uses the setting—Christmastime in an orphanage—to emphasize the emotion.

> What we did not want for Christmas were wristwatches. What we did not want for Christmas were bars of soap. We did not want any more candy canes, bookmarks, ballpoint pens, or somebody else's last year's broken toy. For Christmas we did

not want plastic crosses, dot books, or fruit baskets. No more
handshakes, head pats, or storybook times. It was the night
before Christmas Eve, and Michael Christian had not mentioned *The Birds* in days, and I had given up on the walnut
trains. We did not want any more Christmas wishes.

Richard Yates uses concrete details to illustrate the despair of his
character Warren Mathews after his wife leaves him in the story "Liars
in Love." The precision of language and fact makes me almost weep.

He was tall and very thin and always aware of how ungainly he
must look, even when nobody was there to see—even when
the whole of his life had come down to sitting alone and fooling
with a cardboard toy, three thousand miles from home. It was
March of 1953, and he was twenty-seven years old.

EXERCISES

1. Write a one-page descriptive passage or scene that juxtaposes a
time of contentment with a time of despair.
Objective: To use comparison to illuminate both emotions.

2. Choose a holiday or special occasion, such as a birthday party,
a wedding, Thanksgiving, as the setting to illustrate despair. Write a
scene that shows the contrast between what should be a joyful time
and the despair the narrator feels.
Objective: To learn, by contrasting setting with a character's emotional self, how the elements of fiction work in concert to convey
emotions.

3. Try to write a scene of despair with humor. Use first-person point
of view so the voice is believable.
Objective: To avoid the maudlin or sentimental.

EXCITEMENT

If there were an emotion I would like to bottle and call upon from time to time, excitement is it. And if there were ever an emotion that embodies emotion, excitement is it. In physics, a state of excitement is something at an energy level higher than the ground state. That is excitement, and that is emotion in general. Something more than the status quo, a feeling of something about to happen. Excitement almost has a sound to it, a hum. If it were tangible, it would be electricity, crackling through our bodies.

When we are excited, we are put into motion, stirred to some kind of activity, either literally or figuratively. And since excitement arouses us, it can be sexual as well as emotional. Excitement is a different state of being.

I think of the first time I took my niece to see a Broadway musical. She was eight and the play was *Singin' in the Rain*. I remember the moment just as the lights dimmed, and the audience grew hushed, and the thick maroon velvet curtain parted. I looked over at Melissa and saw something on her face I had never seen before. Yes, her eyes were shining and her hand gripped mine. But more than that was the excitement of being there, of what she was about to experience right in front of her. Even though she loved every minute of the play— especially when it rained on the stage and the actors and actresses bellowed, "We're singin' in the rain . . ." as they splashed through puddles—nothing quite matched that moment of excitement when the play was about to begin. Melissa and I saw many more wonderful musicals together, and she was always happy to be there. But the truest form of excitement was that first time. I will never forget that moment and the way she looked.

Have you felt it yourself, waiting for the boy you love to come up the front walk? Or when the 747 is about to take off and carry you across the Atlantic? Or in the seconds before you dropped to your knee and asked someone to marry you? That is the feeling you need to capture when you convey excitement in fiction.

As with all emotions, beware of the minefield of clichés you must cross in evoking excitement on the page. Everyday people in TV commercials show excitement for toothpaste, chicken nuggets and soap. All of this false excitement makes it difficult for writers to evoke the genuine feeling. Readers, too, are more guarded about how much excitement they will believe.

BAD EXAMPLES

> Ali was so excited she could hardly stand it. She was really going to see Rod Stewart live!

It isn't enough to tell us a character is excited; you need to show us. The writer doesn't let us feel Ali's excitement. What does she do when she's "so excited she could hardly stand it"? How does she feel? How does she act?

> Stephanie felt the proverbial butterflies in her stomach as the train huffed to a stop.

This writer uses a cliché—butterflies in the stomach—to describe excitement. But by calling attention to the fact that it's overused— "the *proverbial* butterflies in her stomach"—she hopes she can get away with it. It's still a cliché, and a fresher image would serve the emotion and the writer much better. Being aware that you're using a cliché does not excuse your using it. If you find yourself saying that something is the "proverbial" something, cut the line and push for a fresher "something."

> Wow! Danny Botticelli was on the phone! For Glory! This was way exciting! Maybe even the most exciting thing that had ever happened to Glory!

The language and exclamation points are overdone. This is written in third person but has none of the distance that point of view demands. If Glory was describing her own excitement, some of this might be effective, as is the second of the "Good Examples." Here, the writer is forcing the emotion.

GOOD EXAMPLES

The simplest way to show excitement is physically. Because it is a real state of being, it does make us feel different physically than we usually feel. The challenge is to describe it in a fresh way—no butter-flies in the stomach! Suzanne Strempek Shea offers us this little gem in her novel *Selling the Lite of Heaven* in which she gives us two physical manifestations as well as an honest attempt at trying to con-trol the emotion.

> My heart did that little flipping thing: I had an invitation to Eddie's mother's home. "I do have some time today," I said, trying to sound like I had to fit her in. "I'll be over after lunch." Not that I expected to be able to eat—I just needed time to prepare myself.

In the next example from the same novel, Shea throws all control away. The language and even the punctuation personify the emotion. But note how the emotion remains rooted in the character. The author is still in control.

> This was it! We were going down the hall! There had to be a bedroom—Eddie's bedroom—down there somewhere. I would see it. Maybe even stand in it. Maybe even lean against the chest of drawers that once held his clothing. Maybe, just maybe, even touch the same exact bed he had slept on for so many years.

In her short story "Carried Away," Alice Munro captures both the combination of emotions that add up to excitement—fear, misgiving and thrill—and a beautiful description of what excitement feels like, how it is a moment of pure emotion. The reference to the world's "crackling" gives a physical presence to the excitement, makes it tan-gible and real.

> Now she felt what everybody else did—a constant fear and misgiving and at the same time this addictive excitement. You could look up from your life of the moment and feel the world crackling beyond the walls.

EXERCISES

1. Make a list of as many cliché physical descriptions of excitement as you can think of. Now start a list of fresh ways to describe excite-

ment physically. Remember Shea's heart doing "that little flipping thing." How many can you come up with?

Objective: To practice avoiding clichés by first recognizing them and then moving beyond them to fresh language.

2. Choose a moment of excitement: the moment before a character walks down the aisle to get married; the moment before a couple first sees the baby they are about to adopt; the moment before a high diver performs in the Olympics; the moment before a young man or woman loses his or her virginity. Now describe the moment without controlling the tone or voice, the way Shea does in describing the excitement at seeing Eddie's bedroom. Use dashes and exclamation points. Make the language giddy and full of hope and anticipation.

Objective: To practice letting language personify the emotion.

3. Now take the same moment and write it with great control. How will you show the reader the emotion without spilling it all over the page? Look at both the first Shea example and the Munro example for ideas.

Objective: To control your writing without losing the emotion.

FEAR

Every night my three-year-old son, Sam, appears at my bedside, afraid. Ghosts, he tells me. Or bad guys. Or a mouse that tried to climb down his throat. All the child development books assure me that three is when children develop fears like this. Monsters and boogeymen and all varieties of scary creatures. It doesn't help to tell them there's nothing to be afraid of, that ghosts aren't real or mice don't want to climb down throats. "What difference do it make," Toni Morrison asks in *Song of Solomon*, "if the thing you scared of is real or not?"

Once a person knows fear, reason can't help. "Fear has a smell, as / Love does," Margaret Atwood wrote in her 1972 novel, *Surfacing*. I like that sensory face for this emotion. One of our jobs as writers trying to convey the emotion of fear is to translate that smell into words. If indeed fear visits us when we are as young as three, then this is one emotion we should be able to revisit in ourselves to help us put it honestly in our fiction.

Growing up in an Italian-American household, I stayed up nights listening to my aunts and grandparents telling stories about "the old country." Those stories were vivid with frightening details: children born with gilis and scales, mysterious illnesses coming and going, candles igniting themselves, witches meeting in olive groves. I would go to bed with all the lights on, afraid to let my legs droop out of the blankets, afraid to close my eyes, afraid of everything. That is one kind of fear I can conjure to help me write the emotion convincingly.

Still another is the fear I felt the night I was mugged at knifepoint on a dark, deserted street in New York City, just four blocks from my apartment. I believed that the thief would kill me as easily as let me go. In fact, he seemed to be deciding what to do. I used that moment of fear when I wrote a carjacking scene in my novel *The Properties of Water*. In the "Good Examples" section that follows, I'll explain how I drew from my real life and turned it into fiction.

What I think is wonderful about writing the emotion of fear is that none of us are strangers to it. To write it convincingly, we need to look inward at our own experiences and then dig into our character's personality to see how we can translate our experience into his. Marilyn Ferguson described fear this way in *The Aquarian Conspiracy*, and I believe this holds the secret to writing fear well: "Just as the seed of health is in illness, because illness contains information, our fears are a treasure house of self-knowledge if we explore them."

BAD EXAMPLES

Shaking with fear, Dottie stepped forward.

Get the cliché police for this one. Shaking does describe what someone might do when afraid, but the phrase is so overused it doesn't work anymore.

Greta was afraid of walking in there, of what she would find. It was like walking into a haunted house at an amusement park. Or down a dark street late at night alone. Or spending the night in a big empty house all by herself.

One of these similes could convey fear. But the author feels uncertain that she's being effective. Piling on similes diminishes the emotion's effect rather than strengthening it.

Lenore was a scaredy-cat. And now Josh felt like Lenore must feel all the time.

Here the writer circles the emotion. He gives us a kind of third-hand route to fear rather than taking time to explore what it feels like for each character. Even if earlier he had explained Lenore's fear, now the writer is relying on an emotional shorthand.

GOOD EXAMPLES

Fear is one emotion that does manifest itself physically. But there are too many easy clichés to describe that physical reaction. I like the description Margaret Halsey uses in *With Malice Toward Some*.

My knees could have been stirred with a spoon.

In *The Good Mother*, Sue Miller conveys the fear of two characters in one scene. Anna finds her young daughter, Molly, terrified at having awakened alone in the car. As the adult, Anna can put words and meaning to both of their fears, but Molly's response is purely physical.

> "Molly," I whispered, and pulled her to me as I clambered in. Her body began to shape itself to mine, to cling to me, even before she really woke up. "Molly," I said. "Molly." And then suddenly, with consciousness, her grip tightened, and she started to cry, screaming in sharp pain like a child who's just fallen, who's bitten her tongue, who's put her hand on a hot kettle, who's lost.
>
> "Mommy!" she screamed, she cried, and held me tighter even than I held her. "Mommy! Mommy!" she shrieked as she would over and over in my memory of this moment.

(Note: Look at the third good example under "Resignation" to see how Anna's fear led to a different emotion.)

Remember my own experience getting mugged just four blocks from my apartment? What struck me most about that was how safe I felt just seconds before it happened. I walked the route from the subway to my apartment at least once a day. Although it was late at night, I had certainly walked those streets even later on other occasions. I was coming from a party at the home of close friends and feeling especially warm and full of good cheer about them and my relationship to them. I felt both physically and emotionally safe and secure. When the man jumped in front of me wielding a knife and demanding my money, I couldn't even quite understand what was happening. In fact, for a fleeting instant I thought I knew him and that he was not threatening me but simply approaching me familiarly.

My character Josie in *The Properties of Water* is emotionally in a similar place at the time of her carjacking. As a wife and mother in a small town, her feelings radiate from her relationship to her husband and children and her home. I made her attack occur at a place where she felt safe: the local shopping mall where her husband manages a department store and where she shops frequently. Emotionally, she is feeling secure and happy. I took my fleeting thought that I knew my attacker and gave it to Josie as a way to build her fear.

As she left the store and walked across the parking lot, balancing her oversized bags, she found herself humming an old song, one from when she was young. . . . By the time Josie reached her car, she was singing it softly to herself, the words coming back to her easily after all this time. . . .

"Excuse me," someone said from behind her.

She jumped slightly, startled. "Oh," she said, turning, her car keys shining bold and silver in the fluorescent light. She hadn't noticed before how this lighting made everything look so eerie. "You scared me," Josie said.

He smiled when she said that, and the smile seemed familiar. . . . Josie lifted her hand to shield her eyes from the fluorescent parking lot light. Will always told her to park under the lights. She glanced around a little nervously. It was amazing how quickly the mall had emptied out. . . .

"I'll take those," the man said, moving toward her, reaching out.

Up close like this, Josie wasn't sure she did know him. His face, which had seemed almost baby-like in the store, seemed harsher out here. Maybe he had been one of those boys in high school that hung out in the parking lot with their souped up cars. . . .

"The keys," he was saying. He moved closer still, so close she could smell him, a mixture of mint mouthwash and soap. . . .

"Are you from East Essex?" Josie said, pressing against the car door. She could feel the hard edges of the door handle in her back.

The man leaned in to her and, to her horror, Josie felt his erection against her crotch. Ridiculously she thought of junior high dances, of boys with greasy hair and too many pimples doing the same thing. . . .

"I know you," she said, "don't I?" She was pinned between him and the car. She couldn't get away.

He was twisting her arm now, twisting it hard so that the keys dropped from her hand. She watched them fall, watched him bend and scoop them up. Even if she screamed there was no one to hear.

EXERCISES

1. As I said earlier, fear is one emotion that really does have physical responses. The weak knees fear can give us are transformed by Margaret Halsey into knees that "could have been stirred with a spoon." Make a list of physical responses to fear. Then list at least ten fresh ways to describe these physical manifestations of fear.

Objective: To show the physical reaction to fear in a way you haven't read before.

2. Look at the example from *The Good Mother*. When Miller describes Molly's fear, it is purely physical. She clings, cries, screams, tightens her grip, holds even tighter, shrieks. But Anna describes her daughter's fear "like a child who's just fallen, who's bitten her tongue, who's put her hand on a hot kettle, who's lost." Choose a situation from the list below:

- an adult runs to help a child whose bike was just stolen
- a mother comforts her child during a thunderstorm
- a parent reassures a child after a nightmare
- a teacher gives bad news to a young student

Now write one paragraph that shows how the child in the situation shows fear and how the adult describes that fear.

Objective: To show emotion through different points of view and to practice showing emotion through both internal and external means.

3. Describe in as much detail as possible a situation in which you felt fear. Reread it, underlining key elements—a repetitive thought you had, a smell or taste that dominated the scene, how you felt just prior to feeling afraid. Translate those key elements to fiction. Perhaps you already have a scene in something you're working on and need to realistically convey fear in your character. Use these elements there. Or write a one-page scene from the point of view of one of the characters listed below using your real-life experience as it would be pertinent to that character and that situation.

- a teenager who has just survived a plane crash
- a bank teller during a robbery
- a mother who realizes her house is on fire
- a man whose car breaks down in a dangerous neighborhood
- a woman alone at night who hears footsteps behind her

Objective: To use your own emotions fictionally.

FONDNESS

In *The Second Common Reader,* Virginia Woolf wrote: "Intimacy is a difficult art." Trying to capture the emotion of fondness in our writing is that same difficult art. It involves intimacy, yes. And a kind of love. But it is not passion or desire. It is not as dramatic as the emotion of being in love. Fondness is more like old jeans—there is a comfort to this emotion, a worn-in feeling.

Whom do we feel this toward? It is true that sometimes we start off liking someone and then fall in love with them. Or develop a sexual passion for them. But there are some people whom we just genuinely like—Great Aunt Alice, a next-door neighbor, a mother-in-law. Mostly, we like our friends. And if, while trying to capture this emotion, you can keep at the forefront of your mind how you feel toward your friends, if you can focus on that type of intimacy, you won't go over-board and drop into some heavier emotion.

In a way, fondness is almost the opposite of passionate love; it depends on different things. In her book *Friendship,* Francine du Plessix Gray called it "the bond least affected by striving for power, physical pleasure, or material profit, most liberated from any oath of duty or of constancy."

Besides confusing fondness with a stronger, riskier emotion—such as passion—the other danger is to understate it. You must be careful not to give it too little emotional verve. If you do that, you will cheat your characters—and your readers—of an important emotion. If you've ever lost or had to throw out your favorite old jeans, you know how valuable they—like fondness—can be.

Emily Dickinson wrote this in a letter, and I think it best sums up the emotion: "I felt it shelter to speak to you." Shelter protects us, makes us feel safe, gives us security. Unlike more dramatic emotions such as passion or hate that can make us feel unsure, unsteady, in danger, fondness creates the feelings that shelter gives. It is a positive but quiet emotion and must be written with care.

BAD EXAMPLES

> Robin! Stuart thought. And he thought it all the time. Robin-RobinRobinRobinRobin! Could it be he had finally found the girl of his dreams?

Although this indicates a sorting out of emotions—"Could it be . . . ?"—it doesn't let the reader consider fondness. This feels closer to love, passion, even infatuation, than it does to fondness.

> They sit together, eating their separate dinners—he tuna salad, she soup. Neither speaks. When they're done, they wash their dishes, retire to the living room and their books—he a biography of a long dead president, she an English mystery.

I think the writer was aiming for comfortable companionship, which could convey fondness. But this feels too emotionally aloof, too dispassionate. There is nothing here to indicate that these two like each other—or that they ever did.

> Stella likes Rob. She likes the way he handles the customers. After all, who else can spend ten hours a day smiling at cranky, unsatisfied consumers? Stella knew, and Rob knew, that The Wacky Warehouse sold junk. But Rob never let on to the customers that he knew. He'll go far here, Stella thought as she watched him grin at a scowling lady.

Stella admires Rob's ability to do his job. But this example doesn't tap into the emotion we're discussing. Admiration is not necessarily achieved through fondness. This is an external device rather than internal character development. Rob's abilities will somehow affect this plot, I suspect. But I don't think it will inform either character's emotional life.

GOOD EXAMPLES

Stephanie Vaughn's short story "Dog Heaven" deals with, in part, the alienation that army brats feel as they move from place to place. The following passage from that story really embodies what Emily Dickinson wrote: "I felt it shelter to speak to you." Here, the young narrator describes her friendship with—her fondness of—Sparky Smith.

> Sparky Smith and I spent our school time smiling too much and running for office. We wore mittens instead of gloves, because everyone else did. We made our mothers buy us ugly knit caps with balls on top—caps that in our previous schools would have identified us as weird but were part of the winter uniform in upstate New York. We wobbled onto the ice rink, practicing in secret, banged our knees, scraped the palms of our hands, so that we could be invited to skating parties by civilian children.

Antonya Nelson explores the differences between fondness and loving in this paragraph from her novel *Talking in Bed*.

> "I *do* like you." Paddy had been about to tell her he loved her. . . . But he wasn't sure he did love Rachel. Maybe it was age creeping up on him; maybe that thing he used to call love he wanted to name something new, such as affection or friendliness. Well, that was ridiculous, he told himself, he was more than affectionate or friendly in his attitude toward Rachel, but was it love?

Let's not forget that sometimes "liking" is the springboard to another emotion. Here is how Cathleen Schine describes "liking" in her novel *The Love Letter*.

> She had instantly decided to like Johnny, but then she had barely noticed him. Johnny the college boy. What does a college boy look like these days? she wondered now. . . . Why, he's got Jeanne Moreau's mouth, she thought enviously. I like him, she decided again. I like having Jeanne Moreau's mouth around.

EXERCISES

1. It is not uncommon for two people to bond because they are different from everyone around them, like Stephanie Vaughn's two young army brats in "Dog Heaven." Below are some ideas of other people in such a situation. Choose a pair—or make up one of your

own—and then write a paragraph that explains their bond and their mutual liking:

- two college freshman away from home for the first time
- two racially or ethnically different kids in a neighborhood
- two new daughters-in-law in a large family
- the only two homosexuals in a corporate office
- twins

Objective: To explore one reason we might like someone.

2. Using a first-person narrator, write one or two paragraphs in which a character is trying to decide if he is fond of or loves someone. Then have a character decide if what he feels is fondness or lust.

Objective: To illuminate the differences for yourself by having a character mull over how these emotions are different.

3. Make a list of all the qualities you like about someone. Cathleen Schine's character likes Johnny's Jeanne Moreau mouth. Don't hold back on this one. Picture someone you really like and list everything you like about her.

Objective: To explore the lighter side of this emotion.

FORGIVENESS

I have a friend who says with a certain amount of pride that she never forgives anyone anything. Cross me, she says, and we're done. I suppose I should say that I *had* a friend like that, because without the possibility of forgiveness, I was bound to "cross" her and the friendship was doomed to end.

Remembering this makes me realize that there have been times when I have found something unforgivable. In college, I walked down a hallway and overheard my roommate telling another girl how much she didn't like me. Another time a friend went to my boyfriend to help me get insight into our rocky relationship and ended up sleeping with him.

But then there have been other times when much larger infractions have occurred and I forgave. Not necessarily easily, but slowly and through gaining understanding and compassion. A friend who did not help me emotionally in the months after my brother died is still a friend, forgiven after years of coming to see that she felt too inadequate to do anything for me. A lover who broke my heart was forgiven after the source of his departure was finally explained.

Thoughtless remarks, callous actions, bad behavior. What is really unforgivable? In writing forgiveness in our fiction, we must understand many things—the act itself, the person who committed it, and the character who is forgiving. We must be sure this emotion, more than perhaps any other, has a larger, understandable context or it will never be believed.

If I told you I know someone whose boyfriend left her pregnant, after planning the pregnancy with her, to go back to his ex-wife and that this woman not only forgave him but married him, you might not believe me. Or you might dismiss her as a ninny, him as a jerk, and the marriage as a sham. But if I gave you context—the ex-wife took his daughter two thousand miles away to break up the relationship, the girlfriend had refused to marry him in the first place—you might reconsider.

Forgiveness, Christina Baldwin wrote in *Life's Companion: Journal Writing as a Spiritual Quest*, is the act of admitting we are like other people. Finally, that may be what you have to ask of your character: Is he at the point in his emotional development to admit he could have made the same mistake? Is he ready or able to forgive?

The key to showing forgiveness in your fiction is to show its motivation within the character. We must be convinced that this character is ready to forgive and is capable of it. If the character forgives easily, we are unconvinced or we think the character is weak or shallow or a saint or some other mistaken notion. Be aware of what forgiveness says about your character. Does it show strength? Largeness of heart? Weakness? Insincerity? Or does the act of forgiveness seem believable given what you have shown us about this character?

BAD EXAMPLES

> Sarah stood before her husband without shame, smelling of her lover and sex and betrayal. "I forgive you," her husband said, moving toward her.

This is a perfect example of forgiveness not ringing true. Instead of us gaining empathy for the husband, we see him as a real loser. Why does he forgive her so easily? The writer may want us to see him as large-hearted, a martyr, of sorts. Instead, we see him as weak and needy.

> Should I forgive him? Jillian wonders as she watches Paul scurrying about to pick up the pieces of broken glass. It was, after all, a family heirloom lying there in shards. But, she reminds herself, twirling a strand of hair around her finger, it was from Aunt Lilly, the old witch. But it looked so good in the foyer. Jillian sighs, decided. "It's okay," she says, only a little reluctantly.

A forgiveness of sorts, but this gives us no insight into the real emotion. Jillian is being frivolous and even toying with Paul. The image of her "twirling a strand of hair around her finger" reinforces this reaction. This scene certainly illuminates her character, but it doesn't inform the emotion of forgiveness with any real depth.

> It had been twenty years since the two brothers had faced each other—or their past. Spalding would never forgive Hank, or their mother, or Marlene. But Hank's arms were opened wide, his face soft.

This reads like the start of something that could give us insight into forgiving. A lot depends on point of view—Spalding is not ready to forgive, so I'm not sure we can understand Hank unless we go into his point of view. Again, this begs for context. What happened twenty years ago? Should Spalding be more forgiving? Why is Hank ready to forgive now? What does each character's stance on the issue say about him? Which stance should we as readers support?

GOOD EXAMPLES

Ray Bradbury portrays forgiveness in one of the most lovely ways possible. Before you read the example below, go to the section on "Shame" and read the passage from his story "Bless Me, Father, for I Have Sinned," in which an old priest goes to confession on Christmas Eve to gain forgiveness. The priest he talks to is another old man, and his confession is what you have just read. Now read how delicately Bradbury illustrates forgiveness.

> Almost without thinking, he raised his hand and made the sign of blessing. The reflection in the mirror did likewise.
>
> Then the old priest, wiping his eyes, turned a last time and went to find the wine.
>
> Outside, Christmas, like the snow, was everywhere.

Mrs. Connolly, a high school English teacher in Kevin Canty's novel *Into the Great Wide Open*, reaches the end of her rope one day in class when she discovers that no one has read the assigned book. Her disappointment is strongest in the teenage protagonist, Kenny, and she sends him out of the room. That act and her forgiveness lead to the brink of a larger understanding for Kenny. Through interior monologue, the reader is able to follow Kenny's emotional progress.

> She was angry with him, Kenny realized—him in particular, for no reason he knew about. And this baby punishment,

sit-out-in-the-hall, this was meant for him alone; and Mrs. Connolly was momentarily visible, human and mysterious, before the eyes of the class got through to him and he real- ized they were watching.

"Sure," Kenny said, and gathered his things, and went out into the hallway; and both of them knew, as they passed each other, that this wasn't what they were talking about, this wasn't what either of them meant. Events, they couldn't be unmade. Put the toothpaste back in the tube. Mrs. Connolly looked at him finally as the door closed: I'm sorry.

In my novel *Places to Stay the Night*, the main character, Libby, leaves her husband and two children and moves to California when the story opens. Through the course of the novel, we see why she left and how her leaving affects her husband, Tom, who still loves her. We get their history together and how they live their lives apart. At the novel's end, Libby asks to come home, and Tom forgives her. Hopefully, all of the context that precedes that act of forgiveness makes the reader accept Tom's decision.

But Libby didn't want to go yet. She said, "I just remembered something else. I remember how you came after me when I left for New York that time before we got married. How you swept me off my feet and the next thing I knew I wasn't in New York at all, I was standing in front of a justice of the peace, shaking like crazy and marrying you." As she said it, she real- ized she was shaking now too. "I don't think I knew what hap- pened until about the third inning of that game we went to at Fenway afterwards."

"That was some day," Tom said, and she knew by the way he sounded that he was remembering too, that it was something they still had together, something that could not be erased.

EXERCISES

1. Read numbers one and three in the "Bad Examples" section for "forgiveness." Choose one of them. Write a page that will lead to that scene. Be sure you give the scene context. Why is Sarah's husband so eager to forgive her infidelity? What happened twenty years ago to Spalding and Hank? When you have written your scene and have

connected it to the given example, be sure to smooth transitions so they read in concert.

Objective: To give the emotion of forgiveness a believable context.

2. At the end of *Places to Stay the Night* we believe that one of the reasons Tom forgives Libby is because they have a history together that is larger than the act of her leaving him and their children. What other reasons can you think of for a character to forgive someone? Below is a list of acts. Come up with a reason to forgive each of them. Don't repeat your reasons.

- infidelity
- a slap across the face
- reading someone else's mail
- taking money from the wallet of someone you don't know
- taking money from the wallet of someone you do know
- wrecking someone's car while driving drunk
- burning down a house
- accidently killing someone
- killing someone intentionally

Objective: Forgiveness relies a lot on cause and effect for its believ-ability. Here you can practice thinking about this connection.

3. Ray Bradbury never uses the word *forgive* or *sorry*. Yet we know that the old priest has been forgiven. What words does he use? What words or images can you come up with as metaphors for forgiveness? Choose two and write a paragraph using them in which the reader understands forgiveness. Do not use the word *forgive* or *sorry*.

Objective: To practice using metaphor.

GRATITUDE

I am always surprised by the things my three-year-old is grateful for. He accepts Tonka trucks stoically but hugs me effusively for making him breakfast. He doesn't blink when I show him the carefully selected Batman Halloween costume I special-ordered, but says, "Thank you!" with great enthusiasm when I tell him we need to go to the post office.

Like everyone else's, Sam's gratitude is a personal emotion. Our job as writers is to convince our readers that the character's gratitude is authentic, and that her reasons for feeling it are true.

In fiction, it is easy to show a character's gratitude for the obvious: the casseroles brought to a home after a funeral, the hug when someone is crying. More difficult—and more interesting—is showing gratitude for the unexpected. A character's gratitude for the something surprising is a wonderful way to develop the reader's understanding of that character. A wife who feels gratitude because her husband makes dinner one night lets the reader in on a lot about her and her marriage. A character who shows gratitude for rain or sunshine or warm weather is giving the reader hints about who he is.

We can also use gratitude to show more than one emotion. Depending on how the writer depicts that wife who is grateful for her husband's cooking dinner, the reader might also see love or resignation or apathy or a combination of several emotions. Since it is so character specific, gratitude is one of the emotions that works well with other ones.

Gratitude can also represent something larger than the obvious act a character appreciates. Because we, and our characters, are grateful for seemingly simple acts or gestures or words, the writer can use gratitude as a kind of "tip of the iceberg" emotion. What is really going on here? the reader might ask when that wife is grateful for something so simple as a dinner.

Gratitude is a tricky emotion because simple thanks are so obvious that we can be fooled into thinking this emotion is one-dimensional. Beware: It isn't.

BAD EXAMPLES

> Paige takes the birthday present and unties the big hot-pink bow, hoping the whole time that Malibu Barbie is waiting inside. She lifts the lid. It is! Malibu Barbie! "Oh, thank you!" she says happily.

This reminds me of my student who wrote a story about a woman who wanted to hear some good jazz. So she takes a cab downtown, goes to a renowned jazz club, and hears some good jazz. No suspense, no dramatic tension, no surprise. Paige wants a Malibu Barbie and she gets one. Is gratitude really so simple?

> "Thanks," Jason mumbles.
> "Speak up," his mother says, nudging him with her toe.
> "Thanks," he mumbles again, staring down at the twenty his father has given him. Any minute now, his father will walk away, like always, as if twenty dollars can buy him his freedom from Jason.

The word *thanks* is certainly representative of gratitude. But here, it illustrates something else: pain, despair, disappointment, maybe even anger or hate. There are buzzwords for emotions: *I'm sorry* can mean forgiveness, but on its own isn't enough; *thanks* or *thank you* can mean gratitude, but as shown here that's not always true.

> Alicia stood at the door of the 727. "Thank you for flying with us," she said to one passenger, to ten, to one hundred and ten. "Thank you for flying with us."

This would actually be a terrific use of irony if it were an example of an emotion other than gratitude. Alicia isn't grateful to these passengers; she's just doing her job. If we had a different context, this could illustrate revenge or disgust or any opposite emotion with irony. But it doesn't show gratitude.

GOOD EXAMPLES

In these two short paragraphs from her story "Rules of the Game," Amy Tan does an awful lot with gratitude. First, she lets us believe that the mother is really grateful for the church Christmas gift of a chess set, even though it's used and missing a black pawn and a white knight. Then she shows us that the mother's pride has been hurt. Finally, we see that the children truly are grateful.

> My mother graciously thanked the unknown benefactor, saying, "Too good. Cost too much." At which point, an old lady with fine white, wispy hair nodded toward our family and said with a whistling whisper, "Merry, merry Christmas."
>
> When we got home, my mother told Vincent to throw the chess set away. "She not want it. We not want it," she said, tossing her head stiffly to the side with a tight, proud smile. My brothers had deaf ears. They were already lining up the chess pieces and reading from the dog-eared instruction book.

Kevin Canty shows the complexity of gratitude in this passage from his novel *Into the Great Wide Open* in which the emotionally awkward Kenny has just looked at some photographs his girlfriend, June, took. He does express gratitude, but what he feels is a different, larger kind of gratitude.

> "No," he said. "I mean, thank you. Thank you for showing these to me, it's like you trust me. I'm just trying to think of what to say."
>
> And it felt like one of those moments—grace, the Holy Spirit—when something told him the right thing to say, and he said it, and it worked.

John Cheever shows gratitude in his story "Goodbye, My Brother" by setting up a contrast between the narrator and his brother. His brother sees the ugliness in everything. When the narrator realizes this part of his brother, he is grateful he is able to see beauty and grace. Contrasting different perspectives is a good technique for illustrating gratitude.

> Oh, what can you do with a man like that? What can you do? How can you dissuade his eye in a crowd from seeking out the cheek with acne, the infirm hand; how can you teach him to

respond to the inestimable greatness of the race, the harsh surface beauty of life; how can you put his finger for him on the obdurate truths before which fear and horror are power-less? The sea that morning was iridescent and dark. My wife and my sister were swimming—Diana and Helen—and I saw their uncovered heads, black and gold in the dark water. I saw them come out and I saw that they were naked, unshy, beau-tiful, and full of grace, and I watched the naked women walk out of the sea.

EXERCISES

1. Can you think of a time when someone else's negative feelings made you feel grateful for something, the way Cheever's story shows one brother aware only of imperfection so that the other brother is grateful for beauty? I remember witnessing a Christmas when a rich teenager was dissatisfied with her plethora of expensive gifts, which made me grateful for my more modest, but heartfelt and appreciated, presents. Write about an experience you've had like that.

Objective: To explore the complexities of gratitude by examining its opposite.

2. I admire the way Amy Tan tricks us into believing the mother's thankfulness, but then ultimately does show us gratitude through the children in the story. Imitate that spectrum of the emotion. Write a scene in which we believe a character is grateful, discover she really isn't, then end with a different character showing gratitude.

Objective: To practice learning from other writers how to explore the subtleties and twists and turns of an emotion.

3. Reread the first bad example for gratitude. Rewrite the scene so it has tension and complexity that allow Paige's gratitude to feel more authentic.

Objective: To use context and tension to give the emotion believa-bility and authenticity.

GRIEF

We tend to think that grief has just two faces: the dramatic wailing and carrying-on face and the stoic, repressed face. But grief covers a whole spectrum of feeling. And we can't predict how grief will show itself to us until it strikes.

Last Valentine's Day, my beloved cat, Lewis, died. He was ten years old and in good health. Our attachment dated back to the April afternoon when he was born in the closet of my studio apartment in New York City. The fourth of six kittens, Lewis emerged pure white and still. In fact, I thought he was stillborn. Before I could decide what to do with the body, he came to life. And from then on, it was love.

Grief is the feeling we get when we lose something or someone we love. And when Lewis died last year, I didn't start to scream, I didn't turn a cold face from his lifeless body. My grief felt more like love—my knees got weak and my heart raced and I started to sweat. These clichés of describing love are an interesting way to describe grief. I sat on the sofa and my arms actually ached from the knowledge that I wouldn't hold that cat again.

I know what you're thinking: *She's writing about grief and she decides to tell us about a cat?* But that is just one face of grief. Here is another. Thirteen years ago, alone in a hotel room in Los Angeles, I got a phone call telling me my brother was dead. He was thirty years old and in good health. When I first picked up the phone and my friend said he had some very bad news, I hung up and sat in the bathroom. When the phone started to ring again, I didn't pick it up. Someone was dead and I didn't want to know who. As long as I didn't pick up the phone, everyone was safe and alive. Of course I eventually took the call and got the news and even got on a plane back east. But what I remember most is sitting alone listening to that phone ring.

But when we write about grief, we don't think it might be about love. We don't think it might be about denial. We only see it as something black and white: Grief is very emotional or grief is very repressed. But people grieving do unexpected things. A man in my childhood town never took down the Christmas tree that was up when his daughter died. A woman I heard about took pictures of her dead baby in the casket and hung them in her parlor. I read about a couple who, after their young son died, adopted two little girls to completely change their lives. These are all the faces of grief in its unpredictable and illogical rendering.

BAD EXAMPLES

When Ellen got the news that her husband was dead, she screamed and screamed until her voice went hoarse; then she screamed silently.

Mrs. Wilcox did not even blink an eye when the policeman came to her door to tell her that her only child had been killed. She simply nodded and went back inside, where she made the appropriate phone calls and waited for her sisters to arrive.

At the funeral, Debra threw herself on the coffin, sobbing.

The above examples are tired and predictable. We've seen grief depicted in these ways too many times. Although one could argue that people do act this way "in real life," it's important to always remind ourselves that fiction is *not* real life; it's a representation of real life. The way people talk and act in real life often seems contrived and false in fiction.

GOOD EXAMPLES

In his short story "Heartache," Anton Chekhov tells the story of the cabdriver, Iona Potapov, whose son has just died the week before. Throughout the story, Iona tries to share his grief with everyone he encounters, but no one will listen. Chekhov demonstrates how grief is both personal and universal.

Iona was silent for a moment, and then he went on: "That's how it is, old girl. My son, Kuzma Ionich, is no more. He died on us. Now let's say you had a foal, and you were the foal's mother, and suddenly, let's say, the same foal departed this life. You'd be sorry, eh?"

The little mare munched and listened and breathed on his hands.

Surrendering to his grief, Iona told her the whole story.

In Michael Cunningham's short story "White Angel," a grown man tells us the story of the events leading up to his teenage brother's death running through a sliding glass door when the narrator was nine. He manages to show how the pain of this emotion is longlasting and intense. Cunningham depicts the narrator's grief, years later.

> I'm grateful to her for holding my brother while he died, but I never once heard her mention the fact that though she had been going through something terrible, at least she was still alive and going places. At least she had protected herself by trying to warn him. I can appreciate the intricacies of her pain. But as long as she was in Cleveland, I could never look her straight in the face. I couldn't talk about the wounds she suffered. I can't even write her name.

The passage demonstrates the depths of grief, but Cunningham goes even further. After reading the last line, we become aware that he has never once used—"written"—the girl's name.

In my novel, *Somewhere off the Coast of Maine*, I tried to render grief by using the experience of my brother's death. Here is how my own experience translated into fiction in a scene in which Claudia's young son, Simon, drowns in a pond in their yard. I wanted to capture several facets of grief and to avoid the clichés we see in the bad examples. To do so, I relied on several rules of fiction: Use concrete details (the particular vegetables, the color yellow, the draperies in the living room), use point of view (I juxtaposed Claudia's memory with what other people told her), and use action (her son's death was so painful she believes she acted in a certain way, a way that works against all the clichés).

> Later, people told Claudia that she, too, had run down to the pond, right behind Elizabeth. They said that she stood screaming at the edge of the water as Elizabeth pulled Simon out and tried to breathe life into him. But she was sure that they were wrong. She had stayed in the garden and picked the lettuce and then the summer squash. An ambulance came and still she kept picking. But don't you remember running up the

hill, holding Simon's hand on the stretcher and Elizabeth yelling for the children to go inside the house? they asked her later. She had looked up, she remembered, when they put him in the ambulance, then she had resumed picking the summer squash. They, too, were a rich yellow. And it was then she had thought of the draperies in the living room. She didn't leave the garden until Elizabeth came and led her away. "No," they told her later. "You ran down to the pond and rode in the ambulance all the way to the hospital." But she shook her head.

EXERCISES

1. Write a one-page scene in which a man or woman is told his or her spouse is dead. Instead of relying on an obvious response to grief, choose a different emotion to demonstrate how the character shows grief. Other emotions you might use are guilt, relief, excitement, hate. Or think of one of your own.

Objective: To explore another face of grief.

2. Choose an obvious way to demonstrate grief. Then take that cliché to a believable emotional place. For example, my character Claudia did respond in a way that might seem cliché, but I juxtaposed her real (perhaps obvious) actions with more surprising actions she later imagined.Write a one-page scene in which a character either throws herself on the coffin of her loved one or sits stoically in a chair as she gets the news of a death. But juxtapose that with something surprising. Suggestions: a celebration of some sort in the background, the arrival of good news, or an imagined action.

Objective: To use clichés believably.

3. Write a one- or two-page scene in which a grieving character is forced to interact with the real, nongrieving world. For example, a widow must go to the Social Security office to get papers on her husband's employment history and the clerk is an uncaring bureaucrat. Or think of your own idea. How would grief show when one is expected to act normally? What physical actions might the character display? Avoiding people's caring stares? Chattering incessantly? How would the person dress? Rely on descriptions that the outside world would take note of.

Objective: To use external descriptions to render an emotion.

GUILT

"Guilt is the one burden human beings can't bear alone," Anaïs Nin wrote in *A Spy in the House of Love*. Perhaps that is why guilt is such a common theme and the emotion that motivates characters in so many fine stories and novels. It is a natural reason for a character to tell, or shape, a story. He is compelled to confess and unburden himself.

Guilt is taking the responsibility for wrongdoing. Or for perhaps even something larger—breaking a law, committing a sin. We have characters who are adulterers, murderers, liars, cheaters, thieves. Often, a story is shaped around a guilty character who feels remorse or finds redemption at the story's end.

Sometimes, however, simply confessing to or revealing the wrongdoing (or sin or crime) *is* the end of the story. This implies that true guilt is never really relieved. The character gives us her side of the event, demonstrates the guilt, but cannot be unburdened. Which is explained beautifully in Mary Shelley's *Frankenstein*: "Ah! it is well for the unfortunate to be resigned, but for the guilty there is no peace."

Much great literature is centered on a moral dilemma and a character's response to that dilemma and to his actions during it. But sometimes we writers shy away from putting our characters in real moral danger, never mind allowing them to actually be guilty of something immoral or wrong or illegal.

Notice that in the first two stories under "Good Examples"—"In the Cemetery Where Al Jolson Is Buried," by Amy Hempel, and "The Girl on the Plane," by Mary Gaitskill—the writers have placed their characters in real moral dilemmas. The choice each character makes leads to a lifetime of guilt. Neither is redeemed at the end. But, as Nin wrote, they have unburdened their guilt on other human beings. In Gaitskill's story, the guilty man tells his story to a woman sitting next to him on a plane; in Hempel's, the narrator tells us, the readers.

BAD EXAMPLES

> My heart is ripped apart by guilt. I will never be the same again.

The weight of guilt is not so easily confessed or explained. It is too complex an emotion for such glib self-awareness. For this reason, the reader doubts the confession. This character simply *wants* to feel guilty, perhaps as a way of forgiving himself for whatever he has done.

> I told Andrea everything—about the other women, the secret savings account, the weekends in Vermont without her. Once the words left my mouth a tremendous weight was lifted from me. I felt free for the first time in years.

Such easy redemption! But in truth, guilt might never lead to redemption. This might work if the narrator confessed but still felt shamed or weighted or even hollow.

> I left the hospital, my own words still ringing in my ear: Use no heroic measures. I didn't know if that's what Dan would have wanted. But it's what I wanted, to be free of him lying there, blank and still. My guilt was like a rock in my belly.

This is a terrific moral dilemma for a character to be thrust into. But her feeling of guilt is too one-dimensional. Part of that guilt would be her desire to sleep late instead of rushing to the hospital. Or her relief that the ordeal is finally over.

GOOD EXAMPLES

The narrator in Amy Hempel's short story "In the Cemetery Where Al Jolson Is Buried" cannot stay with her dying best friend while she dies. In fact, she leaves her to die alone. What follows is a description of that moment of deciding to leave. Later, she will admit that if she told people she had done the right thing and stayed, no one would know the truth. Hempel turns around the cliché of twisting hands by pointing to it as a cliché.

> "I have to go home," I said when she woke up.
> She thought I meant home to her house in the Canyon, and I had to say No, home home. I twisted my hands in the time-honored fashion of people in pain. I was supposed to

offer something. The Best Friend. I could not even offer to come back.

I felt weak and small and failed.

Also exhilarated.

In this excerpt from Mary Gaitskill's short story "The Girl on the Plane," the guilty man is trying to hide his guilt from his wife, and perhaps even from himself.

Her face rose away from her glass in a kind of excited alarm, her lips parted. "You had group sex when you were a teenager?"

"Oh. Not really. Just a gangbang once."

She looked like an antelope testing the wind with its nose in the air, ready to fly.

"It wasn't rape," she said.

"Oh, no, no." Her body relaxed and released a warm, sensual curiosity, like a cat against his leg. "The girl liked it."

"Are you sure?"

"Yeah. She liked having sex with a lot of guys. We all knew her, she knew us."

The opening pages of Leo Tolstoy's *Anna Karenina* are filled with expressions of guilt by Oblonsky, whose wife has just discovered that he was having an affair with the French governess. I strongly suggest reading those pages because Tolstoy uses every device to convey Oblonsky's guilt. The one I've chosen here is my favorite. In it, Oblonsky's reaction is completely opposite to the emotion (guilt) he feels.

He couldn't manage to put on the right expression for his situation with respect to his wife now that his guilt was exposed. Instead of acting offended, making denials or excuses, asking forgiveness, or even remaining indifferent—anything would have been better than what he did do!—his face quite involuntarily (a reflex of the brain, he thought; he was fond of physiology) suddenly took on its usual goodhearted and therefore silly smile.

EXERCISE

1. What is the worst decision you can imagine making? In Amy Hempel's story, it is leaving your best friend to die alone. Write a

scene that shows a character making a moral decision that will leave him guilty for the rest of his life. Remember, that at the point of deciding, Hempel's character feels "weak and small and failed. Also exhilarated."

Objective: To show how the roots of guilt are not necessarily in evil, and that guilt, like all emotions, is a complex blend.

2. When the man in Mary Gaitskill's story denies to his wife that he raped someone, we can assume he is already guilty and is denying his guilt even to himself. Write a scene in which a character is trying to convince someone he is *not* guilty of something he did indeed do.

Objective: To show someone's guilt through his denial.

3. Take the same character you used in the above exercise and have him confess his guilt to a different person. How does he feel after the confession? Relieved? Embarrassed? Does he feel unburdened or does he still feel his guilt?

Objective: To explore the complexities of the emotion of guilt and to see whether a confession leads to redemption or not.

HAPPINESS

This morning I woke up and looked out my bedroom window and felt happy. Yesterday's snowstorm and last night's freeze left all the trees coated in ice, like crystal. The sun glistened through them. And the sun reflected through the stained glass piece that a friend sent me as a thank-you gift—two intertwined hearts. I settled back under my double layer of covers, happy.

Why not content? Happiness is more momentary. It is not as complete. I cannot honestly say that this morning I felt content when I looked out that window: I have morning sickness, a deadline looming, and I need to find a baby-sitter for tonight. Not everything is in place in my world. But for a few moments this morning, those other things felt removed and I could say I was happy.

I think, too, that we trust contentment more than we do happiness. Perhaps because we know happiness is more fleeting, more of the moment. "Happiness," Mary O'Hara wrote in *Thunderhead*, "hangs by a hair." If you are happy now, something will come along to change it. Contentment is more pervasive, more trustworthy. It is an occasion rather than a state of being.

Still, think of how glorious happiness feels! We feel a physical response to it, not unlike excitement. In fact, in *From the Mixed-up Files of Mrs. Basil E. Frankweiler*, E.L. Konigsburg describes happiness like this: "Happiness is excitement that has found a settling down place, but there is always a little corner that keeps flapping around." It is the way we feel dressed up like a grown-up for the first time, waiting for our prom date to arrive; or how we feel when we look down at our home pregnancy test and it is, at last, positive; or how we feel when we open that letter with the good, long-awaited news inside.

Happiness makes us sweat, tremble, jump, squeal, shout. Perhaps because it is, as Anna Pavlova described in *Pavlova: A Biography*, "like a butterfly which appears and delights us for one brief moment, but soon flits away," we give in to happiness more and are eager to let it take us over.

To write well about happiness, we must evoke its fleeting nature as well as what motivates the feeling of happiness. The reader must understand why the character is happy to fully share the experience. The feeling must be special, must be rooted firmly in the character. It is helpful, too, if the reader has seen the character experience other emotions, such as sadness or despair. The happiness, by comparison, will seem more vivid.

BAD EXAMPLES

I was walking on air.

Or "My heart leaped." Or "My heart pounded against my chest." Or any other cliché we've heard over and over again. These expressions do not evoke a real sense of happiness. They flatten the emotion and make it less particular to this character.

I was so happy when I looked into my baby's eyes for the first time.

It is predictable that this moment would lead to happiness. The writer needs to show happiness from an unpredictable moment. I remember how the sight of my baby's perfect ankle made me almost weep; one doesn't immediately associate ankles and happiness. The ankle makes the emotion unique to me and more effective to a reader.

Hillary was happy, happy, happy! She skipped out the door and down the steps, humming a little aimless tune. What a day! What a wonderful, wonderful day! She admired the sparkle of the diamond in the sunlight before she danced into the car and settled all comfy into the driver's seat, grinning.

A problem with happiness is it can be too over-the-top. That's what happens with Hillary. At first, I thought she was a child. The writer's choice of words—skipping, humming a little tune—implied immaturity. The word repetition—"happy" and "wonderful"—and all the exclamation points diminish real emotion. Hillary does not seem happy; she seems simpleminded or childlike. Remember to keep *your* composure when your character is deliriously happy. You must not let the emotion overwhelm the story.

GOOD EXAMPLES

This simple description by Ellen Gilchrist in her short story "The Stucco House" perfectly captures happiness, not just in the language she uses, but in the fact that we know that when Teddy wakes up, happiness might very well be gone.

> Teddy slept happily in his bed, his stuffed animals all around him, his brothers gone, his dreams as soft as dawn.

We don't usually think of Scrooge, from Charles Dickens' "A Christmas Carol," as showing happiness. Yet when the Ghost of Christmas Past takes him back to a long-ago Christmas, Scrooge expresses happiness better than anyone. What makes this so successful is its contrast with the bitter, miserable Scrooge and the exposition we get before Scrooge's excited cries. That exposition prepares us for what's to come so that Scrooge's "heightened" response is believable.

> To hear Scrooge expending all the earnestness of his nature on such subjects, in a most extraordinary voice between laughter and crying; and to see his heightened and excited face, would have been a surprise to his business friends in the City, indeed.
> "There's the Parrot!" cried Scrooge. "Green body and yellow tail with a thing like a lettuce growing out of the top of his head; there he is! . . . Halloa! Hoop! Halloo!"

Here is how a character in Ron Carlson's short story "The H Street Sledding Record" describes his happiness at his and his wife's decision to have another baby. Unlike Scrooge's expression of happiness, Carlson's is understated, relying on warm, familiar words and phrases such as "marriage," "daughter," "my yard," "my very own home," "love," and "Christmas."

> And that's about all that was said, sitting up there on Eleventh Avenue on Christmas Eve on a sled which is as old as my marriage with a brake that is as old as my daughter. Later tonight I will stand in my yard and throw this year's reindeer droppings on my very own home. I love Christmas.

EXERCISES

1. Write fifteen to twenty physical descriptions of happiness. Avoid clichés such as "walking on air." Concentrate on moments of happiness in your life. How are they unique to you, just as my baby's ankle was to me?

Objective: To find fresh ways to describe happiness, an emotion that can be expressed physically.

2. If the Ghost of Christmas Past visited you, where could he take you to cause as much happiness as Scrooge felt in the example? Write that scene: Where and when has the ghost brought you? And how do you show your happiness at returning there?

Objective: To use your own experience and memory to conjure an emotion.

3. Ron Carlson takes Christmas, a predictable time for happiness, and makes us look at it anew through the eyes of his happy narrator. Choose another happy occasion and write a scene that breathes new life into it. Or, if you prefer, portray a happy narrator at a time or occasion that we don't assume is a happy one.

Objective: To make happiness fresh.

HATE

When I was growing up, only a few words were banned from our household. We could not call each other liar. We could not say we were starving, because we always had food. And we could not say, "I hate you." Hate, we were taught, is the worst possible emotion to feel. To hate others was to wish them dead, to dismiss their value. When you hate, we were told, you become part of what you hate.

In *The Mask of Apollo*, Mary Renault wrote the same sentiment: "In hatred as in love, we grow like the thing we brood upon. What we loathe, we graft into our very soul." Like other emotions we've discussed, hate is not a simple, flat feeling. In fact, to know hate we must also know love. "Love commingled with hate is more powerful than love. Or hate," Joyce Carol Oates wrote in *On Boxing*.

At the Bennington Writers Workshop I heard the poet Liam Rector say that to hate is to at least feel something; it is worse to feel nothing at all. Passion is part of this emotion too. It is intense and consuming. But it can also be short-lived. However, when we feel it, we feel it with every part of our being.

Han Suyin once said that she could only hate for five or ten years. "Wouldn't it be terrible to be always burdened with those primary emotions you had at one time?" A primary emotion is a good way to think of hate (and love and grief and happiness, to name a few). So basic to our being, so deeply felt, it sometimes hurts to remember the source of such a feeling. But to write it convincingly we must find it again in ourselves.

BAD EXAMPLES

"I hate you!" Jill shouted.
"I hate you too!" Barbara shouted back.

The two women walked off in opposite directions, neither looking back.

It isn't enough to have characters simply say what they feel. And the actions—shouting and storming off—aren't that illuminating either. How do Jill and Barbara show hate? What do they feel? How do they feel it?

> Penelope watches as Simon sleeps. The unruly lock of hair that always falls into his eyes is pushed back for once, and she can see the curl of his lashes, the beginnings of crow feet. He has done it again. Left her waiting up, alone, all night, imagining the worst. Diane would tell her that the worst would be that he was dead somewhere; but Penelope knows better. The worst is that he is with someone else, whispering the same lies, pretending the same feelings. The worst, Penelope thinks, is probably exactly where he was. "I hate you," she whispers into his ear, stroking his arm lightly. "I hate you."

This scene definitely shows an emotion, but that emotion doesn't feel like hate to me. Even though Penelope uses the words, the actions and thoughts lead the reader to a different emotional place.

> Cody had had enough. Hate bubbled through his veins, scalding his heart, his soul. He picked up the crowbar, and moved toward her. "You rotten bitch," he spat.

Okay. Cody is definitely angry. And I believe he hates this woman. But this is an easy way to demonstrate hate—pick up a crowbar and, we assume, beat someone with it. I can't argue that this excerpt doesn't demonstrate emotion, but the writer could use less cliché and more thought.

GOOD EXAMPLES

"I tell you," Willa Cather wrote in *The Song of the Lark*, "there is such a thing as creative hate!" Creative hate is how I see what Jill McCorkle does in the following passage from her novel *Tending to Virginia*. The main character, Virginia, is pregnant and unhappy. McCorkle uses hating the color yellow as a way to show us how strongly Virginia is feeling about her life and her situation.

And, she hates yellow. She wishes there was absolutely nothing yellow in the entire world. "Yellow is perfect for a nursery because it can go either way—boy or girl, yellow," the tennis guy's wife had said. Screw her, impregnate her, paint her life yellow.

In his short story "The Model," Bernard Malamud shows us hate in the way a young woman responds when she believes an old man has impersonated a painter simply to get her to undress in front of him. After she has dressed again, she asks him to undress so she can paint him naked.

Mr. Elihu disrobed, ashamed of how he must look to her. With quick strokes she sketched his form. He was not a bad-looking man but felt bad. When she had the sketch she dipped his brush into a blob of black pigment she had squeezed out of a tube and smeared his features, leaving a black mess.

He watched her hating him but said nothing.

Ms. Perry tossed the brush into a wastebasket and returned to the bathroom for her clothing.

There are few times in our lives when we feel emotions as intensely as we do when we are teenagers. Everything feels exaggerated, from our love of Paul McCartney to how unjust the world is. Therefore, a teenager's hate is dramatic and heartfelt and intense. Maggie, from my novel *The Properties of Water*, is filled with emotion. Here is a scene in which, unable to show just how much she hates her family, she does an outlandish, perfectly adolescent thing. This act brings freshness to the emotion and makes it particular to Maggie.

Maggie jumped off her bed and stamped her feet hard.

"Me? A princess?" she shouted. "Me? I don't get anything in this house except your old smelly bedroom, and no one listens to me, and I could be dead up here for days and no one would even notice I was missing!" She yelled loud, but she knew they didn't hear her because her father was having a full-fledged allergy attack, sneezing like crazy, and Kate was singing "Do, Re, Mi" even louder than she'd been singing before and her mother was banging dinner on the table.

"I hate you!" Maggie yelled. "All of you!"

Frustrated, she looked around for something to throw or break, but all she could see was her ugly dried-up corsage. She yanked it from the wall and, without thinking, ate it, all the dead petals disintegrating on her tongue, tasting like nothing but dust.

EXERCISES

1. Ms. Perry, from "The Model," and Maggie, from *The Properties of Water*, both show hate through actions. Ms. Perry smears paint over a sketch until she has a black mess. Maggie eats her dried corsage. The verbs used to describe these actions are strong, just like the emotion they are conveying—"squeezed," "smeared," "tossed," "throw," "break," "yanked." Also, both of the actions are surprising. Avoiding cliché and remembering to use strong active verbs, write a scene in which a character acts out her hate.

Objective: To use a strong physical act to show hate.

2. The color yellow becomes a symbol for all the things Virginia hates about her life in *Tending to Virginia*. Imagine a character who hates his situation. What is that situation? Why does he hate it? Now choose an external thing to focus that hate on. McCorkle used a color, so don't choose that. Write a paragraph in which the hated thing helps the reader to understand what the character is really feeling.

Objective: To practice using metaphor to show emotion.

3. Read the example from Carson McCullers' story "A Domestic Dilemma" on page 118. Remember that hate has roots in its opposite emotion—love. Earlier in the McCullers story, Martin imagines the morning after, when his alcoholic wife, Emily, would feel ashamed and humiliated by what she'd done the night before and would repeatedly call him at his office.

> He felt that his secretary had divined the trouble long ago and that she pitied him. He suffered a moment of rebellion against his fate; he hated his wife.

Write a paragraph that describes a man's love for his wife (or a wife's love for her husband). Then write another paragraph that describes his hate for the same character. Emily is an alcoholic. Remember to give your character's spouse a flaw too—perhaps drug addiction, adultery, even abandonment. Make sure both paragraphs are equally convincing emotionally.

Objective: To explore the complexities of emotions.

HOPE

In *Outrageous Acts and Everyday Rebellions*, Gloria Steinem warns that "Hope is a very unruly emotion." To writers trying to capture that emotion in their work, it can seem very unruly indeed. On the positive side, hope brings to mind optimism and faith and even expectation of good things. In fiction, however, trying to convey such feelings can sound too sentimental.

In my novel *Places to Stay the Night*, I had a character named Renata Handy who was the single mother of a dying five-year-old girl named Millie. Not to be crass, but dying children in fiction are fair game for sentimental writing. Add a single mother whose own life is so wrapped in her child's and I was on very dangerous territory. Of course I wanted Renata to hope her daughter would be cured. But how to make that hope seem believable rather than maudlin?

As with all emotions, to convey hope requires looking past the obvious. I've read far too many scenes in which a mother prays to God to save her child, or weeps over the child as he lies in a hospital bed. Of course in real life, these scenes can be moving and common and painful, but on the page they lose their power. One way to show an emotion is to have the character deny or repress her own feelings. In one scene, after Renata hears Millie's diagnosis, she responds, "There's been a mistake." Later, she notices that other children have dolls and pajamas and teddy bears and other things from home with them in the hospital: "But Millie was only here for the night, she reminded herself. She didn't need anything like that."

Renata's denial is even stronger because of the type of character she is before her daughter's illness: strong, no-nonsense, and practical. She does not believe in fairies or guardian angels or myths and fables. But when Millie is in the hospital, Renata tells her that thunder is "The angels . . . The angels are bowling." This effort to satisfy the child's love of the fantastic and to admit to a higher being of some sort was for me the best way to show Renata's hope that her daughter might get well.

"Hope is a strange invention," Emily Dickinson wrote in a letter to Mabel Loomis Todd. And it is. Hope is what keeps some of us going every day when others might feel despair; it can motivate us, sustain us, even save us from the world or from ourselves.

BAD EXAMPLES

> "I hope this baby's a girl," Lucy said, rubbing her belly and looking at the cheerful Winnie the Pooh mobile she'd just hung.

Using the verb "hope" doesn't capture the emotion of hope that we're talking about here. How often in a day do we say, "I hope . . ." to not be late, to see a certain someone, that the grocery store is still open or the movie we want to see is still playing. That kind of hope is more wishful, less intense than the emotional hope we want to convey.

> Jenny hoped for many things—world peace, an end to hate, nuclear disarmament . . .

This tells us what kind of person Jenny is rather than conveying the emotion that hope can embody. Although emotions help us define characters, here the character seems already defined—either a Miss America contestant or a hippie in 1969. Also, these hopes are vague and abstract and so lack a direct link to the character.

> Georgia knew her husband would get well; he had to. He was everything to her. Her lover, friend, soul mate. He would survive this. He would.
> "Mrs. Eldridge?" the nurse said. "The doctor needs to talk to you now."

This does convey hope, but it is too melodramatic. This writer has fallen into the trap I discussed earlier. In life, a person might very well think these thoughts and feel these emotions. But in fiction they read false, probably because we've read or heard them so many times already they've lost their power.

GOOD EXAMPLES

The narrator of James Baldwin's story "Sonny's Blues" uses a child's point of view to describe a scene in which a mother who has died is remembered. Like curiosity, hope is an emotion that is natural for children to convey.

> Maybe there's a kid, quiet and big-eyed, curled up in a chair in the corner. The silence, the darkness coming, and the darkness in the faces frighten the child obscurely. He hopes that the hand that strokes his forehead will never stop—will never die. He hopes that there will never come a time when the old folks won't be sitting around the living room, talking about where they've come from, and what they've seen, and what's happened to them and their kinfolk.

Like other emotions, we might think of hope only in grandiose terms, as if our characters were superhumans who only hoped for large things. But Laura Kasischke, in her novel *Suspicious River*, shows how real and sometimes sad hope is when she describes her small-town character's seemingly small hopes of working in a shopping mall.

> I'd walk down the gray tunnel of that mall between J.C. Penney's and Sears and imagine one day I'd work at one of those department stores, when I got tired of the motel, or fired. Maybe I'd work in Lingerie. I'd imagine myself wrapping pink silklike slips in tissue paper and slipping them into my purse when the manager took her coffee break.
>   At that mall, I always felt dimly full of hope for the future. Someday, I thought, I'd get a job there.

The title character in Gloria Naylor's "Kiswana Browne" sends her hopes on a metaphorical journey. Metaphor is a good technique for giving emotion and the story itself depth and complexity.

> A pigeon swept across her window, and she marveled at its liquid movements in the air waves. She placed her dreams on the back of the bird and fantasized that it would glide forever in transparent silver circles until it ascended to the center of the universe and was swallowed up.

EXERCISES

1. Flip back to the section on despair. Read the quote from Mark Richard's story "The Birds for Christmas." When Michael Christian and the narrator are some of the last Big Boys to go home with someone for Christmas, the narrator tells us they are certain that "*someone* would eventually come for us." He says they "were not frightened yet." The story then moves us from that hope to the despair that you just read. Try writing three opposite emotional scenes of your own. Write first a paragraph describing a character's hope, then a paragraph describing that same character's despair. After you've written three of those, try it with other emotions, such as love/hate, excitement/disappointment, happiness/sadness.

Objective: To practice moving a character from one emotion to its opposite to demonstrate the character's growth.

2. Baldwin re-creates a child's hope from the past. His mother does die, and the old folks no longer sit around the living room. The child is now a man. Knowing this adds a bittersweetness to the emotion. Think back to your own childhood and write a scene in which you are the child who hopes for things that you now know will not be. Perhaps you'll recall the last time all of your family was together, and you hoped those reunions would come every year, and that everyone would be as happy as they were on that day. Be specific. When and where were you? Who was there? What were your hopes?

Objective: To practice the other side of hopefulness—the bittersweet tone of unrealized hopes.

3. Baldwin uses hope to look backward; Naylor uses it to look forward. Kiswana Browne puts her hopes on the back of a bird and sends them upward. This could come across as sentimental, but Naylor makes the reader really feel Kiswana's hopefulness. Where else can a character figuratively place her dreams? Can you come up with one place? Three? Five? Ten? Make sure you do not cross over into sentimentality.

Objective: To practice using figurative language without sentimentality.

HOSTILITY

Hostility is one of those emotions that can really charge the air. It is almost tangible. I think of the years I spent working as a flight attendant when passengers would board the airplane, full of hostility: Their baggage had been lost, there were no window seats, the flight was late and they would miss their appointments. They used to face me, red-faced, eyes fiery, fists clenched, sometimes even raised, as if I were the enemy.

After all, we do call enemy territory "hostile grounds." Perhaps this is a good way to think about hostility when you write it. The hostile character is at war—with another character, a situation, or even himself. Some people demonstrate hostility loudly: "I'll never fly this stupid airline again!" Others show their hostility more quietly: "Just you wait. I'll show you what happens when you lose my bags."

This is true in fiction too. If you want to show hostility in a character, you can do it through dialogue. Or you can use voice, a narrator whose every word oozes with hostility. Or you can show it to the reader more quietly, through a character's thoughts or actions. I like this description in Tillie Olsen's "Tell Me a Riddle": "Vinegar he poured on me all his life; I am well marinated; how can I be honey now?"

What you must keep at the front of your creative mind, though, is that hostility is antagonism. A hostile character sees someone or something as the enemy and is about to go to war. Like so many other emotions, hostility lends itself too easily to cliché. Stop yourself and make sure you are not writing a caricature, but rather a real, hostile *character*.

BAD EXAMPLES

> "I hate you, you jerk!"
> "Well, I hate you too!"
> "Oh, yeah?"
> "Yeah!"

This is certainly hostile, but it doesn't inform us of anything. Dialogue can be one of our most useful tools in showing emotion, if it isn't cliché or obvious. It should be specific and particular to the speaker. These lines could be spoken by anyone. The hostility is generic and ineffective.

> Smith couldn't take it anymore. He had to do something. But he didn't know what. Why did he feel so upset?

Too vague! Is this really hostility? What's causing it? How does it feel to Smith? We need more showing, more concrete details, more careful writing. The emotion is defused by the question. When we're feeling hostile, we rarely are in a mood to question our motives. Smith's circumspection makes me doubt that he can't "take it anymore."

> Tom decided the root of his hostility toward Margaret was her hair: frizzy, bleached, in need of a trim. He couldn't even talk to her without staring at it, angrily.

This writer came close here. Using Margaret's hair as the source of Tom's hostility is good. It strikes an effective and unexpected note. We don't usually think of hair as a cause of hostility. But we don't know if he used to like her hair. What was it like? Was he hostile to her before? Is he threatened by her hair? This writer needs to let us see what Tom and Margaret were like before the bad hair.

GOOD EXAMPLES

The character Joy in Flannery O'Connor's story "Good Country People" is as openly hostile as she can be. Joy is described as "a large blond girl with an artificial leg." Her mother, Mrs. Hopewell, excuses her behavior because of the lost leg. Here is an example of Joy's hostility. Note how O'Connor uses physical description as well as dialogue to show Joy's hostility and defiance.

> . . . and when Joy had to be impressed for these services, her remarks were usually so ugly and her face so glum that Mrs. Hopewell would say, "If you can't come pleasantly, I don't want you at all," to which the girl, standing square and rigid-shouldered

with her neck thrust slightly forward, would reply, "If you want me, here I am—LIKE I AM."

Now look at how Jayne Anne Phillips uses voice to depict hostility in her short story "Lechery." This character's descriptions ooze hostility—Phillip's verb choices, "pummel," "dislodge" and "push," are especially effective.

> Though I have no money I must give myself what I need. Yes I know which lovers to call when the police have caught me peddling pictures, the store detectives twisting my wrists pull stockings out of my sleeves. And the butchers pummel the small of my back to dislodge their wrapped hocks; white bone and marble tendon exposed as the paper tears and they push me against the wall.

In "The Story of a Scar," James Alan McPherson uses dialogue juxtaposed with physical action to illustrate hostility. He chooses an odd catalyst—a scar—to incite the hostility.

> Since Dr. Wayland was late and there were no recent news-magazines in the waiting room, I turned to the other patient and said: "As a concerned person, and as your brother, I ask you, without meaning to offend, how did you get that scar on the side of your face?"
>
> The woman seemed insulted. Her brown eyes, which before had been wandering vacuously about the room, narrowed suddenly and sparked humbling reprimands at me. She took a draw on her cigarette, puckered her lips, and blew a healthy stream of smoke toward my face. It was a mean action, deliberately irreverent and cold. The long curving scar on the left side of her face darkened. "I ask you," she said, "as a nosy person with no connections in your family, how come your nose is all bandaged up?"

EXERCISES

1. Although Joy's remarks are "ugly," O'Connor uses wonderful physical descriptions to depict hostility. Joy's face is "glum"; she stood "square and rigid-shouldered"; her neck is "thrust slightly forward." Practice using physical descriptions to illustrate hostility. First de-

scribe just a hostile face. Then describe hostile hands. Finally describe hostile eyes.

Objective: To hone physical descriptions so they convey emotion.

2. One of the reasons McPherson's excerpt so successfully portrays hostility is his choice of hostile words: "scar," "insulted," "narrowed suddenly," "sparked humbling reprimands," "puckered her lips," "blew a healthy stream of smoke toward my face," "a mean action," "deliberately irreverent," "cold," "darkened." Choose any three of McPherson's words or phrases, then add seven of your own. Make sure they evoke hostility. Then write a one-page scene that uses all ten.

Objective: To carefully choose language that depicts the emotion.

3. Write a one-page scene of hostile dialogue. McPherson used a scar as a source of the hostility. Choose one of these:

- a fur coat
- a tattoo
- lost car keys
- a bright pink house
- a smelly dog
- bad breath

Objective: To effectively use dialogue to depict emotion.

IRRITATION

Irritations are annoyances. They do not drive you to crazy actions or wild shouting. They simply frustrate you, disturb you, make you uncomfortable, make you sigh or even groan. Here is a list of things that irritate me:

someone reading over my shoulder

traffic

waiting too long for subways or buses

whining

humidity

bad salad dressing

people who don't pay attention

broken answering machines

people who are always late

having to waste time correcting computer problems (with bills, lost articles, etc.)

the blue envelope that holds an overdrawn notice

inappropriate whispering

getting caught in the rain without an umbrella or sensible shoes

running out of hot water in the middle of a shower

Nothing in the above list makes me angry. They just bother me, the way a pebble in your sock rubs against your heel.

Whatever the source of the irritation, the writer must make the reader feel as annoyed as the character feels. That is your goal. Through dialogue or reminiscence or action you want to show the character's irritation so vividly that the reader feels it too.

Depicting irritation well can let something or someone under the readers' skin, rubbing away, forcing them to scratch.

BAD EXAMPLES

> Timothy was so irritating! "Leave me alone!" Marissa said
> angrily. She was fed up with her brother; she'd had enough.

This writer tells us she's showing irritation, but really she goes too far. This is anger. Of course, irritation can lead to anger, but the buildup to that is missing here. The statement that "she'd had enough" is also untrue of irritation. When we reach a breaking point, we've moved beyond irritation into other emotions.

> Every time Gina brought up Kenny, her friend June stopped
> listening. Gina kept trying. She told June about the picnic he'd
> packed, the little notes he left on her desk. But June just started
> talking about the upcoming Christmas party.

This has potential for showing irritation. But it's too expository. We don't hear, see or feel how irritating this character can be. Instead, we get a summary. Written in dialogue, this conversation might be more effective.

> Cassie hated when they talked about people she didn't know.
> She got up from the table and started loading the dishwasher.

This is a good setup for irritation, but the reader doesn't take it anywhere. Cassie hates when they talk about people she doesn't know, but what does that mean exactly? Is she irritated? Or bored? Perhaps she feels left out of the conversation and is mildly hurt by the exclusion. We simply do not know what she is feeling. More specific details would help to convey the feeling of irritation.

GOOD EXAMPLES

In her novel *The Hundred Secret Senses*, Amy Tan creates a character of an irritating sister perfectly. Here is an example of just how irritating she can be.

> She snaps on the light and proceeds to demonstrate, hands on
> hips, twisting at the waist like a sixties PE teacher. I wonder
> how long she's been standing by my bed, waiting for me to
> waken so she can present her latest bit of unsolicited advice.
> Her bed's already made.

> I look at my watch and say, in a grumpy voice, "Kwan, it's only five in the morning."
>
> "This is China. Everyone else is up. Only you're asleep."
>
> "Not anymore."

Since most of us are somewhat irritable when awakened early in the morning, we share the speaker's feelings. Kwan's "twisting" is so oddly self-absorbed that we, too, are irritated by her.

Bone, the narrator of Russell Banks' novel *Rule of the Bone,* shows his stepfather's irritation by explaining it as if in a conversation with the reader. Notice how he uses inflection for emphasis. Also, we come to see that not only is the stepfather irritated with Bone, but Bone feels irritation at his stepfather too.

> My stepfather developed this new habit of referring to me as him and never talking directly to me or even looking at me except when he thought I didn't notice or when he was drunk. He'd like say to my mother, Ask him where he's going tonight. Tell him to take out the goddam trash. Ask him how come he goes around with torn clothes and wearing earrings in his ears like a goddam girl and in his nose for chrissake, he'd say with me watching TV right there in front of him.

In the short story "The Fireman's Wife," Richard Bausch uses dialogue to depict irritation. Look at how the irritation escalates as these two friends talk to each other. By showing the escalation, Bausch increases the reader's involvement in the irritation.

> "Wouldn't you like to have a family?" Jane says.
>
> "Sure."
>
> "Well, the last time I checked, that meant having babies."
>
> "Yuck," Eveline says again.
>
> "Oh, all right—you just mean because of the pain and all."
>
> "I mean yuck."
>
> "Well, what does 'yuck' mean, OK?"
>
> "What is the matter with you?" Eveline says. "What difference does it make?"
>
> "I'm trying to have a normal conversation," Jane says, "and I'm getting these weird one-word answers, that's all. I mean, what's 'yuck', anyway? What's it mean?"

"Let's say it means I don't want to talk about having babies."

"I wasn't talking about you."

EXERCISES

1. Write one page of dialogue between two people that shows increasing irritation in both characters.

Objective: To use dialogue to effectively show emotion.

2. Bone is a disenchanted teenager. This is immediately clear from how he talks. Choose a character type and have her explain someone's irritation to the reader in one paragraph. You can choose from one of the types below or make up one of your own.
- a recovering alcoholic tells about his distrustful wife
- a pregnant woman tells about the unwilling father of the baby
- a sick old man tells about his healthy wife
- a young woman tells about her new boyfriend who is allergic to her cat

Objective: To practice writing in a voice other than your own.

3. Write a one-page character sketch of the most irritating person you can imagine. Then write a three-page story in which that person is stuck in an elevator with you. Write it in first person. Do your best to avoid stating how you feel. Instead, show us.

Objective: To create a believable irritating character by juxtaposing him with someone normal.

JEALOUSY

I can still vividly remember the first time I felt jealousy. I was four years old and at my best friend Maria's birthday party. She appeared in a hot pink dress covered with lime green frogs sitting happily on lily pads. It was, I decided, the most beautiful dress in the world. And I wanted it so badly I couldn't concentrate on anything else. By the time I got home, I was miserable. When I told my mother why, she said, "You don't want a dress like that! It's ugly!" But she was wrong; I did want it. And I knew I wasn't ever going to have it if my mother thought it was ugly. Jealousy had me and wouldn't let go.

In his book *Care of the Soul*, Thomas Moore defines jealousy as simply wanting something that someone else has. That was certainly true with me. But the definition belies the emotion itself, which is large and even frightening. In *Death of an Expert Witness*, P.D. James describes jealousy like this: "Jealousy, he thought, was as physical as fear; the same dryness of the mouth, the thudding heart, the restlessness which destroyed appetite and peace." That comes very close to describing how jealousy feels.

People say, "She was green with envy," as if it actually flows through the bloodstream. When jealousy strikes, that is how it feels. It has a way of consuming us. It can destroy friendships and love affairs. It can make us irrational, drive us to do embarrassing things. That is one reason jealousy is an emotion people are hesitant to admit they feel. It is wrong, we think, to want your friend's job or husband or personality. As a result, we find characters struggling with the emotion—defining it, describing it, admitting it—just as we struggle in real life.

Jealousy feels like a lot of other emotions: anger, frustration, irritation, even despair. It is important to remember that when you try to evoke it in your fiction. And to remember its power to overwhelm us.

In *The Mill on the Floss*, George Eliot wrote, "Jealousy is never satisfied with anything short of an omniscience that would detect the subtlest fold of the heart." Eliot wrote that as if jealousy were a real living thing, and that is how you must look at it to write about it convincingly.

BAD EXAMPLES

She was green with envy.

This and any other cliché, of course, have to be avoided. But jealousy lends itself to cliché, so be extra careful to have your cliché police on the alert.

Jim felt angry and humiliated. He also felt disappointed in Agatha. And in himself. He was sad that he felt this way. But he was also embarrassed that other people might know what Agatha had been doing.

Jim is obviously jealous. But the writer muddles this emotion by mentioning so many others. Although it's true that jealousy is a combination of a lot of emotions and that it feels like anger and disappointment and many others, it would be clearer to focus on one of those as a way to explore the jealousy.

I'm so jealous of Kate, Bettina thought. Kate was prettier and smarter and, worse, Bill liked her.

This feels inauthentic. Jealousy is a difficult emotion to admit, and Bettina does so too easily. The details of *why* she's jealous of Kate are much more convincing than her easy admission.

GOOD EXAMPLES

The strength of this description of jealousy from Joyce Carol Oates' short story "Easy Lay" comes from her use of concrete details rather than vague images or clichéd phrases. She takes a clear, specific approach that gives power to her description.

Girls in my neighborhood were jealous of me the way their mothers and fathers were jealous of my mother with her blond hair, her face and figure and clothes and bronze Cougar.

When we examine jealousy closely, we see that much of it comes from what we don't know; we fill in the blanks as to why our husbands were so late coming home or what they're doing at lunch with their ex-girlfriends. Pam Houston uses the role that imagination plays in jealousy in her short story "How to Talk to a Hunter." This approach brings a wistfulness to the description.

> The next day the sun will be out and the coyote woman will leave. Think about how easy it must be for the coyote woman and a man who listens to top-forty country. The coyote woman would never use a word like "monogamy," the coyote woman will stay gentle on his mind."

Jealousy is so complex it sometimes feels like other emotions. Barry Hannah uses that facet of jealousy in his story "Water Liars." His speaker expresses jealousy through anger. Notice, too, that his jealousy is irrational. He is jealous of the lovers his wife had before he met her. But this type of confusion is typical of jealousy.

> It makes no sense that I should be angry about happenings before she and I ever saw each other. Yet I feel an impotent homicidal urge in the matter of her lovers. She has excused my episodes as the course of things, though she has a vivid memory too. But there is a blurred nostalgia women have that men don't.
>
> You could not believe how handsome and delicate my wife is naked.
>
> I was driven wild by the bodies that had trespassed her twelve and thirteen years ago.

EXERCISES

1. What I most love about the Oates example is the detail of the bronze Cougar. The color bronze—not brown or tan or even copper, but "bronze"—and the sexy type of the car make the mother very real. Make a list of vivid details that would evoke jealousy. Oates began her list with stereotypes: "blond hair," "her face and figure and clothes." Do that too. First, list twenty obvious things that would evoke jealousy. Then, write ten unusual ones. Can you use details from your list to write a few paragraphs from the perspective of a jealous character? Give it a try.

Objective: To move beyond cliché and to use concrete details to evoke emotion.

2. Pam Houston's character in "How to Talk to a Hunter" doesn't really know anything about the coyote woman. She demonstrates jealousy through what she *imagines* the coyote woman is like. Write a one- or two-page scene in which a character is imagining the ex-lover of her husband.

Objective: To explore the complexity of jealousy: It isn't always concrete or based on something (or someone) tangible. It often is unreasonable and confusing.

3. First, write a list of emotions that feel like jealousy and/or emotions jealousy includes. Then choose one of them and write a paragraph describing jealousy through that emotion. In "Water Liars," Hannah demonstrates jealousy via anger. He uses strong words like "homicidal urge" and "driven wild" to evoke both emotions. Which emotion will you choose? How will you convey it and jealousy? Take risks. Choose an emotion rarely associated with jealousy.

Objective: To use another facet of jealousy and to be clear in your description of it.

LONELINESS

Let us not confuse loneliness with being alone. Although I suspect we are often made aware of our loneliness then, being alone is not enough to create it. Certainly we can all remember wonderful times spent alone: rainy afternoons snuggled under a quilt and lost in a good book, long meandering walks filled with window shopping or sight-seeing or daydreaming, even early mornings when we wander outside with a cup of coffee and enjoy a few moments by ourselves. In *Mrs. Stevens Hears the Mermaids Singing*, May Sarton wrote, "Loneliness is the poverty of self; solitude is the richness of self."

When describing loneliness in your fictional characters, that is the distinction to keep in mind. A woman I knew who had broken off her engagement from her long-term boyfriend said that Sundays were the loneliest times for her. The sight of families going to church together and couples eating brunch in cafes, all of the things that Sunday represented, made her sad and reminded her she was not part of a larger thing: family, couple, love.

The most striking proof that loneliness differs from solitude is that loneliness can strike when you are with someone, even when you are in a crowd. I spent too much time in a relationship in which I would cry from loneliness at night as the person slept peacefully beside me. And there have been times when I've sat at Christmas dinner with my large extended family and felt more lonely than I had been sitting alone in my apartment two hundred miles from them.

For writers, loneliness can become an easy way to manipulate a reader's sympathy for a character. Rather than work hard to develop that sense of the poverty of self, a writer can resort to trite—and therefore ineffective—ways to evoke loneliness and hope to win the reader. We can use obvious clichés, such as rainy days, a telephone that never rings, or empty ice-cream cartons to set the stage for loneliness. Or we can make a character weep out of loneliness and rely on that weeping alone to convey the emotion. But the trite and the cliché leave the harder emotional work undone and are never effective. With loneliness, the writer must be especially careful to push past the sentimental and maudlin and find the heart of the character's emotion.

BAD EXAMPLES

> Sarah was home alone for the afternoon. How would she ever spend such a lonely day? Baking and eating a batch of brownies all by herself sounded right. Then she would put on her video of *An Officer and a Gentleman* and cry.

This writer has confused being alone with loneliness. In fact, Sarah might be lonely, but the reader needs more information to be convinced of that emotion. Also, the writer has used easy examples of how loneliness is expressed—eating fattening food and watching a romantic movie.

> Ted knew that if he could only get out, among people—to the mall, maybe—he wouldn't feel so lonely.

We know that one of the worst types of loneliness is the kind felt in a crowd. Perhaps Teddy doesn't know that yet; but it feels like the writer doesn't know it either.

> Tabitha felt scared and lonely, like the last leaf on a winter tree. "I'm lonely!" she told herself.

This writer is guilty of trying too hard to explain an emotion rather than showing the reader how that emotion really feels. A simile like the one above makes us stop: Leaves do not feel lonely. So how can we use that to understand how a character is feeling?

GOOD EXAMPLES

In his short story "A Small, Good Thing," Raymond Carver uses happy images to convey loneliness. We don't often associate loneliness with birthdays and weddings, but Carver expresses the emotion by giving the reader plenty and celebration as a way to intensify the feeling.

> Although they were tired and in anguish, they listened to what the baker had to say. They nodded when the baker began to

speak of loneliness, and of the sense of doubt and limitation that had come to him in his middle years. He told them what it was like to be childless all those years. To repeat the days with the ovens endlessly full and endlessly empty. The party food, the celebrations he'd worked over. Icing knuckle-deep. The tiny wedding couples stuck into cakes. Hundreds of them, no, thousands by now. Birthdays. Just imagine all those candles burning.

Lorrie Moore shows us in her short story "You're Ugly, Too" the loneliness that comes when someone is alone and realizes how lonely she actually is. The character's self-awareness and the humor of the Baggie images help to avoid a feeling of self-pity.

At the movie—*Death by Number*—she bought strands of red licorice to tug and chew. She took a seat off to one side in the theatre. She felt strangely self-conscious sitting alone, and hoped for the place to darken fast. When it did, and the coming attractions came on, she reached inside her purse for her glasses. They were in a Baggie. Her Kleenex was also in a Baggie. So were her pen and her aspirin and her mints. Every-thing was in Baggies. This was what she'd become: a woman alone at the movies with everything in a Baggie.

One of the best ways to show any emotion is to show it indirectly, to have a character deny the emotion when it is obvious to the reader that the emotion is there. Terry McMillan shows loneliness indirectly in the opening paragraph of her novel *Waiting to Exhale*.

Right now I'm supposed to be all geeked up because I'm getting ready for a New Year's Eve party that some guy named Lionel invited me to. Sheila, my baby sister, insisted on giving me his phone number because he lives here in Denver and her simple-ass husband played basketball with him eleven years ago at the University of Washington, and since I'm still single (which is downright pitiful to her, considering I'm the oldest of four kids and the only one who has yet to say "I do"), she's worried about me. She and Mama both think I'm out here dying of loneliness, which is not true.

EXERCISES

1. Write a one-page scene of a happy occasion—a wedding, a baby shower, a graduation. Describe the event from the point of view of a lonely character. How do all the other people look to her? How does the event make her feel? What kinds of things does she do that show us how lonely she feels?

Objective: To use contrasting emotions to help evoke loneliness and to explore how an emotion can change the way a character sees people and events.

2. Write a one-page scene in which a character who is alone is also lonely. Be sure his aloneness is not what defines the loneliness. Remember how Lorrie Moore's character acted in the theatre?

Objective: To differentiate between *alone* and *lonely*.

3. Terry McMillan's lonely character denies her loneliness. Choose another emotion from the list below and write a one-page monologue in the voice of a character who, though she feels that emotion, is denying it.

- anger
- love
- happiness
- fear
- jealousy

Objective: To evoke emotion indirectly.

LONGING

Even the word *longing* gives me an ache in my chest. Longing is a persistent yearning or desire that cannot be fulfilled. Therefore it has, inherent in it, a sadness, almost a mourning. It is what we feel for a lost love; or for a different, perhaps happier, time in our lives; or for people who are far away, or unreachable. We long to be younger, more innocent, more in love, more carefree.

Longing is a little like desire, but it is stronger. When we desire something, we can usually—or sometimes, at least—obtain it. We use the phrase "my heart's desire," which is almost hopeful and light. More likely the thing we long for is out of our reach. And if we somehow can retrieve it, the intensity of the longing does not fade. In *Dream Children*, Gail Godwin wrote: "The act of longing for something will always be more intense than the requiting of it."

Whereas desire is often for a person, longing is more easily associated with a time. I think of how I ached for an old boyfriend when I was unhappy with another relationship. That ache was larger than simply desiring the ex-lover, though. It was wrapped up in a longing for a certain time in my life, when I lived in a particular apartment in a particular city and my life was lived in a particular way.

Although it is true I could have returned to the ex-lover, I could never return to those years and that place we occupied together then. There is not really hope in longing, and that might be why it feels so sad. We know we can't be younger, or more innocent, or many of the other things we long for. "The force behind the movement of time is a mourning that will not be comforted," Marilynne Robinson wrote in her novel *Housekeeping*.

When you try to evoke longing in a character, perhaps you will be closer to the truth if you avoid focusing on desire and hope and instead think of this emotion as a kind of mourning. Mourning carries with it a sadness, a loss, and a yearning that longing shares.

BAD EXAMPLES

> All Jenny could think about was Tom. She wanted to be with him so badly that she could almost smell his spicy scent, almost feel the weight of his arm around her shoulders. Enough, she thought, and picked up the phone and dialled Tom's number.

This is desire, not longing. True, Jenny yearns desperately for Tom, but he is only a phone call away. Remember that longing is not easily fulfilled.

> Patrick thought that if he closed his eyes and wished hard enough, the things he dreamed for might really come true: the bright blue soccer jacket, the train that puffed real steam, a smile from Elizabeth Jenkins next door.

This sounds more like hope than longing. Patrick sounds too young to feel the ache that accompanies longing, and he is so optimistic that he believes wanting something hard enough can make it happen. Longing has more hopelessness to it than hopefulness.

> "I love you," Bill wrote. "I want you more than anything in the world. I need you by my side." Ha! he thought as he read over the words. He crumpled the paper and tossed it in the wastebasket on his way out the door.

There is certainly longing in what Bill wrote, but a reader would not be convinced of that emotion. Bill gives up too easily, too cavalierly, to convey true longing.

GOOD EXAMPLES

Richard Bausch's story "Aren't You Happy for Me?" takes place in one afternoon when a long-married couple are about to tell their daughter they are separating. Instead, the daughter calls them with news of her own that prevents them from sharing theirs with her. At the end of the story, the husband is struck with a profound longing for a time when they were in love and their daughter was small. Not only is the description here beautifully written, but Bausch uses a memory as a bridge to the character's longing. Like the emotion itself, when the memory fades, an aching remains.

He sat there remembering, like Mary, their early happiness, that ease and simplicity, and briefly he was in another house, other rooms, and he saw the toddler that Melanie had been, trailing through slanting light in a brown hallway, draped in gowns she had fashioned from her mother's clothes. He did not know why that particular image should have come to him out of the flow of years, but for a fierce minute it was uncannily near him in the breathing silence; it went over him like a palpable something on his skin, then was gone. The ache which remained stopped him for a moment.

Arturo Vivante looks at a different kind of longing in his story "Can-Can." A character is longing for something he has but is, perhaps, about to lose. In the story, a man is about to go off and secretly meet another woman when his wife lifts her skirt and does the can-can. The image disturbs him and almost prevents him from going. But he does, and afterward, as he and the woman lie together, they have a revealing conversation.

"What are you thinking about?" she said afterwards, sensing his detachment.

For a moment he didn't answer, then he said, "You really want to know what I was thinking of?"

"Yes," she said, a little anxiously.

He suppressed a laugh, as though what he was going to tell her was too absurd or silly. "I was thinking of someone doing the can-can."

It is easy to think we only long for things that were good in our lives. But Robert Stone shows us a character longing for a drink in his story "Helping." The first few sentences lead the reader to believe the longing is for something good. The final sentence hits us like a slap.

One gray November day, Elliot went to Boston for the afternoon. The wet streets seemed cold and lonely. He sensed a broken promise in the city's elegance and verve. Old hopes tormented him like phantom limbs, but he did not drink. He had joined Alcoholics Anonymous fifteen months before.

EXERCISES

1. Arturo Vivante surprises us when the man in "Can-Can" longs for the wife he has just left behind for a rendezvous with another woman. Write a scene in which a character is longing for something surprising, such as a truant child longing for school or an elderly woman longing for a baby.

Objective: To really examine the emotion itself without using a contrived plot or event to convey it.

2. Both Bausch and Stone write about longing for another time; one longs for a happier time in his marriage, one for a time when he could drink. Choose one of those two topics and write a scene that demonstrates the emotion. Be sure to make the present situation clear and strong to contrast with the time longed for.

Objective: To portray character development—a character is at a certain point in life and longing for a different time. Make it clear why the character longs for another time and how that character has changed for the better and for the worse.

3. Emotions are best understood and conveyed when we can tap into our own emotions. What is the time or person or thing you most long for right now? Write about it as clearly as you can. Describe it with concrete details. Try to really evoke the essence of that time or person through sensory triggers (how did it taste? look? smell? etc.). Write this like it's an entry in a journal. Don't worry about how it works as fiction. Instead, describe it as accurately as possible.

Objective: To use your own experience to better understand an emotion.

LOVE (PARENT-CHILD)

"If you have never been hated by your child," Bette Davis wrote in her autobiography *The Lonely Life*, "you have never been a parent."

That sounds pretty severe when the emotion I'm discussing is parental love. But like any kind of love, the love between a parent and a child is complex, sometimes confusing, and actually a mixture of many other emotions: tenderness, happiness, jealousy, confusion, disappointment, despair. To name just a few.

What I looked for in examples that illustrate this complex emotion were passages that showed parental love with depth. It is so simple to write about how much a mother loves her child. It is a given. But the feeling just isn't that one-dimensional. A parent's love has all the complexity of any emotion. Perhaps it has even more. Parents hang hope on their children. They experience pain and happiness with them and sometimes through them. They worry about them. They delight in them. They get angry with their children, and they get joyful over them.

Like any complex emotion, parental love can be contradictory. As a columnist for *Parenting* magazine, I try to explore all the facets of parenting, many of which are not often discussed. The love and adoration one feels for his child is written about *ad nauseam*. But the feelings of confusion (am I doing the right thing?), of worry (will she be safe?), of anger (put that down *now!*), and a score of other serious, even negative emotions are often neglected by writers. This neglect is not only dishonest, it is shortsighted from a writer's perspective. By exploring the complexity of the parent-child relationship, the writer creates more opportunities for drama.

To convey an emotion honestly and convincingly, you must see it honestly yourself. Parental love is not as simple as it sounds. To really portray it in your fiction you must face it head on. That means a parent acknowledging or accepting her own mixed feelings about her child, and a parent admitting who she is and who her child is. The important thing to remember is that we are talking about parental love. The mix of emotions parental love implies should not negate or even dilute the fact that love is at the heart of what you want to show. Instead, these other emotions make the love more interesting and complex, more human.

BAD EXAMPLES

> The little shit! I couldn't stand to hear her anymore. Not her whining, not her crying, not her simpering voice.

Rather than explore some of the contradictory emotions that are a part of love, this seems to really be about hate. Remember that you can't lose sight of the emotion you are trying to convey, especially when it is such a complex one as parental love. Keep love at the core by controlling the other emotions involved in it. This writer has let frustration overwhelm the love.

> She was my daughter and I loved her more than anything— more than the house we lived in, more than my husband, more than myself.

This is one side of the emotion. But without a contrast to some other side it sounds too sentimental. The speaker sounds weak, as if the love is too strong for her.

> Gail looked down at her newborn son. She loved him! It was all so easy!

Although again there might be a germ of truth in this portrayal of parental love, it is too flat, too simple, too unconvincing. It is, therefore, uninteresting to the reader.

GOOD EXAMPLES

In her short story "Poltergeists," Jane Shapiro beautifully conveys both the contradictory emotions that make up parental love and the overwhelming responsibility that is so much of being a parent.

> I remember standing there on the grass watching Zach and Nora and their friends strolling away. At that moment, as I

might have expected but hadn't, a wave of feeling broke over me; it was an unfamiliar combination—real, deep sadness and heart-stopping relief. I would miss them so much I'd never get over it—I couldn't live without them! At the same time, for my purposes they weren't leaving fast enough. I couldn't wait another minute to start not caring so much.

Barbara Kingsolver says that she wrote her story "Quality Time" to "explore that awful and wonderful thing that happens to parents when life with our children suddenly opens wide in the narrowest passages." The climax of the story comes with a realization by a mother about her young daughter. That realization portrays the depth of parental love.

In the overtones of her voice and the way she pushes her blond hair over her shoulder there is a startling maturity, and Miriam is frozen for a moment with a vision of a much older Rennie. All the different Rennies—the teenager, the adult—are already contained in her hands and voice, her confidence. From moments like these, parents can find the courage to believe in the resilience of their children's lives. They will barrel forward like engines, armored by their own momentum, more indestructible than love.

Those sometimes frightening negative emotions that also make up a part of parental love are well described in the following passage from Roddy Doyle's novel *The Woman Who Walked Into Doors*. Here we see jealousy, anger, the threat of violence.

There were some times when I was so jealous I wanted to maim her, really hurt her. I adored her. She was my pride and joy; still is.

EXERCISES

1. In *The Love Letter*, Cathleen Schine describes a woman's love of her daughter as "a life almost unbearably full, euphoric and miraculously hers." This is the positive side of the relationship. But Schine gets to it by giving her reader a number of seemingly negative examples—pounding feet, whining. Write a paragraph that ends with Schine's line "a life almost unbearably full, euphoric and miraculously

hers." But in the sentences that lead up to that line, have a mother thinking about all the maddening things that describe her son or daughter, actions and habits that we would not usually consider lovable.

Objective: To explore the complexities of parent-child love.

2. Write a two- or three-page scene about a parent watching his adult child enter a new stage of life: a child's wedding, the birth of a grandchild, a bas mitzvah, a prom. What does the parent think about while watching the older child "leave" in a way? What kind of realization might occur?

Objective: To explore the deep feelings and thoughts a parent experiences.

3. Roddy Doyle writes about seemingly contradictory emotions in the same paragraph to convey the depth and complexity of parent-child love. Write five different paragraphs, each one exploring two opposite feelings. For example love and hate, anger and acceptance, despair and joy.

Objective: To explore the complex and contradictory feelings of parent-child love.

LOVE (ROMANTIC)

I cannot think of an emotion that is more complex than romantic love, than that state we refer to as being in love—which always makes me think of jumping head first into a deep body of water. Love is a total immersion emotion.

This emotion has been explored for centuries. Writers have struggled to understand love, to explain it, to express its complexity and depth. Part of the complexity is that love contains a good portion of suffering. We say we love someone so much it hurts. Louisa May Alcott described love like a disease in *Little Women*: "She's got most of the symptoms—is twittery and cross, doesn't eat, lies awake, and mopes in corners."

When we are in love we feel everything more intensely. If we are away from the people we love, certain songs can send us into uncontrollable sobs, the sound of our loved ones' voices can make our hearts pound, overdue phone calls can start fits of depression. George Sand said: "Whoever has loved knows all that life contains of sorrow and of joy." Love is full of such contradictions.

Part of what makes love so complex and contradictory is the importance we give it. How to convey such love then in our fiction, without sounding too sentimental or maudlin? To write about love in a way that sounds authentic rather than cliché is one of our biggest challenges. Love is a hodgepodge of deep and often conflicting emotions—romanticism, power, jealousy, sorrow, hope, loss, desire, lust, hate, fear. We must evoke these contradictions as they are manifest in a particular character at a particular time and place. We have to keep our characters grounded in the story, in the scene, in the feeling.

Close your eyes a moment and remember your first love: How did you feel when you looked at each other? Remember how even the thought of that person could send you headlong into a series of physical reactions? How the mention of your love's name could drive you to distraction? Now, how do you describe all of that to your readers in a way they've never read before?

BAD EXAMPLES

He loved her more than anything.

He loved her like crazy.

He loved her madly.

The above are not just clichés; they don't really tell us anything about love. They rely on the reader's familiarity with the emotion to do all of the writer's work. To write well about this often-written-about emotion, we must seek the fresh, the particular. We must avoid clichés and commonplace statements at all costs.

Her love was like the moon and stars, it was like the great bottomless sea.

Although this writer is attempting to explore love, such abstractions don't really describe an emotion. This ends up trivializing love rather than showing its complexities and depth. The similes are trite and unimaginative and show a writer whose mind and heart are not truly engaged. Is "her love" developed or clarified or made particular in any way? Quite simply: No.

It was just as she always knew it would be—her heart soaring, their hands forever entwined. She was finally, really, in love.

Too sentimental, too inauthentic. How much more realistic and true when we read Jean Rhys in *Quartet* saying: "Love was a terrible thing." Or Marge Piercy in *Braided Lives* claiming that "Love says, mine. Love says, I could eat you up." These statements show us love in a new way, make us nod our heads in agreement. Soaring hearts and "hands forever entwined" don't evoke such agreement. They are generic, greeting-card sentiments that will turn off the reader.

GOOD EXAMPLES

In Eudora Welty's story "No Place for You, My Love," simply by looking at a woman seated beside him at a luncheon, a man decides she is having an affair. Welty uses interior monologue to show the reader how the woman feels about life and to convey romantic love. Using this device helps the reader understand the character by hearing her thoughts on this complex emotion.

> It must stick out all over me, she thought, so people think they can love me or hate me just by looking at me. How did it leave us—the old, safe, slow way people used to know of learning how one another feels, and the privilege that went with it of shying away if it seemed best. People in love like me, I suppose, give away the shortcuts to everybody's secrets.

Joy Williams describes love simply in her story "The Wedding." Yet by giving the lovers almost magical powers she manages to capture how powerful love makes us feel. Using the phrase "their amniotic embrace" conveys a sense of safety as well as unconditional, pure love like a mother feels for her unborn baby.

> Together, in their amniotic embrace, they float out the window and circle the house, gazing down at all those who have not found true love, below.

The complexity and contradictions of love are explored in Carson McCullers' short story "A Domestic Dilemma." McCullers not only contrasts feelings of love with strong negative feelings by using words such as "blame," "blemish," "anger," and "sorrow," but she also calls attention to these contradictions with the phrase "the immense complexity of love." After you have read this example of love, go back and read the example from the same story in the section on hate, from the same point of view, about this husband and this wife.

> For the first time that evening he looked at his wife. His eyes rested on the sweet forehead . . . As Martin watched the tranquil slumber of his wife, the ghost of the old anger vanished. All thoughts of blame or blemish were distant from him now. Martin put out the bathroom light and raised the window. Careful not to awaken Emily he slid into the bed. By moonlight he watched his wife for the last time. His hand sought the adjacent flesh and sorrow paralleled desire in the immense complexity of love.

EXERCISES

1. Carson McCullers states that love is a complex emotion. She then includes anger, sorrow, desire, and lust in her description of how Martin loves his wife. Write a one-page scene in which you do the same. In the scene announce that love is complex. Then choose and illustrate three other emotions that love includes.

Objective: To be direct with your reader in describing an emotion.

2. Now write the same scene *without* naming the emotions you chose. How can you show us a love that includes these three other emotions?

Objective: To show emotion *indirectly*.

3. Read the examples from "A Domestic Dilemma"; notice how McCullers turns the emotion of hate into love. That's what you should do: Take one of the exercises you did for the emotion hate and rewrite it as love. How can an example of hate turn around to become an example of love?

Objective: To explore the contradictions that make up the emotion of love.

PASSION

When I think of passion, the first image that comes to my mind is that wonderful scene from the movie *From Here to Eternity* in which a wave washes over Burt Lancaster and Deborah Kerr as they kiss with wild abandon on the beach. Passion is like that wave—it envelops us, it consumes us, it takes over; and it's like that kiss—all-encompassing, reckless, wonderful.

But beware! Passion is different from obsession although both imply a strong desire. Obsession brings to mind being taken over by the devil or being compulsively fixed on an idea or emotion or person. Obsession produces anxiety.

Passion, however, brings to mind positive feelings—ardor, enthusiasm, love, and, of course, lust. Although it is true that we sometimes say, "I hate him with a passion," that negative connotation is not passion's primary one.

What these emotions share, and perhaps why they can be confused, is that they are both very deep and very strong. In fact, obsession and passion can be overwhelming to the person feeling them. As writers trying to convey passion, we must remember the difference between the two.

An easy way to keep them separate is to think of all the nonsexual things people can have a passion for. Right off the top of my head, I can say that I have a passion for expensive chocolate, the ballet, Paris, pasta, good books, the ocean. If I were obsessed with, say, chocolate, this intense emotion would manifest itself quite differently.

Perhaps a good point to keep at the forefront of your mind when you're writing passion is this line from Eudora Welty's story "Circe": "Passion is our ground, our island—do others exist?" Passion both grounds us and separates us, unlike obsession, which only separates us. But passion also makes us feel like nothing exists but the object of our passion.

BAD EXAMPLES

> All Rosalind wanted was to touch Michael, to feel the warmth
> of his skin next to hers, to taste his mouth, to . . .

You get the idea. Yes, passion can be lustful and sexual. But remember that emotion is a feeling, and in the case of passion, an intense and deep feeling. Describing sex certainly includes passion, but it doesn't necessarily describe the emotion itself.

> It was all Danielle thought about: Marc. She thought about
> him when she was at work, as she drove down Santa Monica
> Boulevard, while she watched her clothes spin dry. Sometimes
> she could not hear what her roommate was saying, or re-
> member a page she'd just read. There was only Marc. . . .

Here's a good example of obsession, not passion.

> Warren picked up the brick and slammed it down on her head
> again, with a passion he'd never known before. She was already
> dead; he knew that. The first three blows had done the job. But
> after what she'd done to him, dead didn't seem enough.

Passion? Maybe. But it sounds like a better description of anger or hate or vengefulness. Remember, just using the word doesn't convey the emotion.

GOOD EXAMPLES

In *That Night*, Alice McDermott captures emotions effectively on every page. This paragraph illustrates passion as it can be felt only by a teenager in love.

> That night when he came to claim her, he stood on the short
> lawn before her house, his knees bent, his fists driven into his
> thighs, and bellowed her name with such passion that even the
> friends who surrounded him, who had come to support him, to
> drag her from the house, to murder her family if they had to,
> let the chains they carried go limp in their hands.

Vladimir Nabokov gives passion a shape in the way he describes a meeting and a kiss in his story "Spring in Fialta." There is a breathlessness to the writing—in fact the excerpt below is all one sentence—that imitates the breathlessness of passion.

> I call her Nina, but I could hardly have known her name yet, hardly could we have had time, she and I, for any preliminary; "Who's that?" she asked with interest—and I was already kissing her neck, smooth and quite fiery hot from the long fox fur of her coat collar, which kept getting into my way until she clasped my shoulder, and with the candor so peculiar to her gently fitted her generous, dutiful lips to mine.

I admit that even the word *passion* brings to my mind love and sex and desire. But remember that many things can inspire passion. Look at how Isaac Babel uses passion for language in his short story "Guy de Maupassant."

> "How did you do it?"
> I began to speak of style, of the army of words, of the army in which all kinds of weapons may come into play. No iron can stab the heart with such force as a period put just at the right place. . . .

EXERCISES

1. Make a list of all the passions of your life. Then make a list of obsessions you've had.

Objective: To see the differences between passion and obsession.

2. Write a one-page description of your own first love.

Objective: To explore how to show an emotion through your own experiences.

3. Remember how I said that Nabokov gives passion a shape in "Spring in Fialta"? The run-on sentence, the choice of words—"fiery hot," "fox fur . . . collar"—remind me of a speeding train. Perhaps they conjure a different image for you. How would passion look? First, make a visual of passion using paints, ink, collage, clay or anything you want. Then write a few sentences describing passion as a palpable object.

Objective: To find new ways to view and explain an emotion by making it three-dimensional.

RESIGNATION

In her poem "I Have Had to Learn to Live with My Face," Diane Wakoski states, "Learning to live with what you're born with / is the process, / the involvement, / the making of a life." This pretty much sums up resignation; it is learning to live with what you're born with, or given, or come across in life. It is an acceptance of that thing, or those things, a giving over or submitting to them.

When trying to depict resignation, remember it is not regret or sadness. When a character feels resignation, she has accepted a turn of events or a course of action or a place in life without regret or sadness. Sometimes you must first take a character through another emotion—such as regret—before she reaches resignation. In fact, this emotion probably seems truer when we have travelled with the character to this place. We can often better understand resignation if we've seen how the person arrived there.

Celeste De Blasis describes it like this in *Wild Swan*: "There are people who live lives little differently than the beasts, and I don't mean that badly. I mean that they accept whatever happens day to day without struggle or question or regret. To them, things just are, like the earth and sky and seasons." Although you might have a character who lives this way, it is more likely that you have a character who is sometimes like this, or becomes this way after a certain point or only in a certain situation.

Therefore, resignation is a good emotion for exploring real character development. A story about a man who gets a fatal prognosis from his doctor or a couple trying to save their marriage can take those characters through many emotions—anger, hope, sadness—to resignation. This is a challenging emotion to convey purely and accurately and a real test, in a way, for writing other emotions well.

BAD EXAMPLES

> The doctor shook his head. "I don't even think in vitro will work in your case, Susannah."
>
> "Thank you for your time," Susannah said, gathering her things. So, she thought as she walked away, there would be no children for her and Paul.

Susannah's resignation is so simple and so complete, we can't help but disbelieve it. Even if the writer did show us other emotions earlier—some hopefulness, perhaps—this still comes too quickly and too easily.

> Robin turned one final time to look at the little yellow house, the place where she believed she would grow old, the place she believed she would never leave. Her whole body ached with the pain of ruined dreams, things gone wrong, missteps and misgivings.

Perhaps Robin has accepted that she is leaving something behind, but this sounds more like regret than resignation. Remember that resignation is different from regret or sadness. As this story continues, we might see Robin reach resignation finally, but it doesn't look like she has yet.

> The thing about Old Man Hinkle was he didn't care. The school kids called him names like Peg Leg and Pirate, his own son hadn't visited since last Christmas, and now his television set had stopped working. So be it, he thought.

Another fine line here: It sounds like Old Man Hinkle is apathetic rather than resigned. How could this writer turn this into resignation, if that is indeed the emotion he is seeking for this character? There are several ways. Perhaps Hinkle doesn't care *anymore*. Adding that one word would show a change in emotion. Or the first line could be deleted altogether. Or a new line could be added to show how Hinkle used to feel, a line that convinces us he is not unfeeling but resigned.

GOOD EXAMPLES

The novel *Push* by Sapphire is in many ways about acceptance. The sixteen-year-old narrator, Precious Jones, pregnant for the second time, displays her resignation to her life in this passage by actually wishing for the alternative. We feel the emotion even though the author makes no specific mention of it. And we feel the pain of this statement because it is straightforward, honest. The speaker sounds truly resigned, but she does not ask for our pity—nor does she pity herself.

> Sometimes I wish I was not alive. But I don't know how to die. Ain' no plug to pull out. 'N no matter how bad I feel my heart don't stop beating and my eyes open in the morning.

Toward the end of Jill McCorkle's novel *Carolina Moon*, the character Mack finally reaches resignation. His young wife, Sarah, is in a coma, and throughout the novel we have watched him grapple with many emotions—despair and hope and anger, to name a few—as he seeks to accept his, and her, fate. In this paragraph, Mack finally reaches the emotional point where he realizes he and his wife will never have the children they longed for, that Sarah will not recover. Notice how McCorkle uses outside events to mirror Mack's internal emotion. His love—and his resignation—are clearly shown in the way he lifts her leg and massages it, in the sounds of children at play.

> He stands in the doorway looking at Sarah, hoping for something, a blink, a sigh. She's too young for this. He sits on the foot of the bed and pulls the covers to the side. Her leg is thin and cool as he lifts it, up and down and up and down. He massages her ankles and feet, rubs lotion into her skin. And outside the voices continue to rise and fall, screams and laughs from the children he has not met. Freeze. You're it.

There is a scene in Sue Miller's novel *The Good Mother* in which the narrator, Anna, accepts that she cannot raise her little girl, Molly, alone. This resignation comes when Anna finds Molly frightened after waking alone in the car in a strange place (see the section "Fear"), and in fact it mirrors the theme of the whole novel: Is Anna a "good mother"? In the following sentence, she seems resigned to the fact that perhaps she is not.

> And I sat hunched in the back seat with her in my arms until she was still, feeling only that I could not do this alone, I was not strong enough, good enough to do this alone, I could not do this.

EXERCISES

1. Rewrite the third bad example so that Old Man Hinkle conveys resignation instead of apathy. I've given a few ways to do this, or you can try one of your own. After you've accomplished this, rewrite example two so that Robin shows resignation instead of regret.

Objective: To distinguish resignation from other emotions.

2. Look again at the first bad example. Keep it as the last paragraph, but write two or three paragraphs to precede it. Make them take Susannah through one other emotion (try despair, hope, regret, loss, or sadness) thoroughly enough to convince us she is at real resignation at the end. You will probably have to tinker with the given paragraph too, but keep it as close to its original form as you can.

Objective: To move a character through an appropriate emotion to resignation.

3. Wallace Johnson, another character in Jill McCorkle's *Carolina Moon*, reaches resignation when he is about to retire from his job at the local post office. Retirement is a natural time for a character to feel resigned. Make a list of other situations that might make resignation believable. Now write one or two lines describing that situation and why the character feels resigned.

Objective: To integrate the emotion with a believable external reason for it.

RESTLESSNESS

When I was a teenager, I used to sit at the top of the steps that led to our upstairs bedrooms and stare out the tiny window there. The view was not spectacular: our driveway with my aunt's Chevy Impala parked in it, the empty street, another aunt's house on a small hill in the distance, and then more of the hills that made up our small New England mill town.

Sitting there, I would play a game of mental escape. I would imagine myself first in the driveway, then crossing that street, then passing my aunt's house, then moving, finally, beyond each of those hills. Where would they lead? All I wanted was to flee from our provincial town. I didn't even care where my escape brought me, as long as it was away. I imagined myself in cities—Boston, New York, London. I imagined myself in faraway countries—Thailand, Australia, Brazil. So deep was my restlessness that later, at night in my bed, I would stare into my dark room and mentally write postcards to all the people I'd left behind.

Restlessness has a motion to it. It's a person constantly tapping his feet or drumming his fingers. It's a kinetic emotion. And at its root lies discontent. We are not restless in our small towns, our marriages, our families, unless we are unhappy there. To write restlessness well, you must keep both of these points in mind: its physical side and its emotional side. How does the character display the kinetic energy of restlessness? What is at the root of the character's unhappiness?

There is an easy way to show restlessness: Simply have a character pace a room or tap a pencil along a tabletop. But that shows not so much the emotion that makes up restlessness as a short-term condition that results in it. A man is in the waiting room pacing while his wife gives birth; someone drums her pencil along a tabletop as she waits for her flight to be called for departure. Then the baby is born, the plane is airborne, and the restlessness is gone.

True restlessness is not temporary. For some people, it never leaves. "Now more than ever," Isabelle Eberhardt wrote in *The Passionate Nomad: The Diary of Isabelle Eberhardt*, "do I realize that I shall never be content with a sedentary life, and that I shall always be haunted by thoughts of a sundrenched elsewhere." Decide if this describes your character, or if the restlessness can be resolved, not by a plane taking off, but by a bigger departure.

BAD EXAMPLES

> Agnes got up and sat down, then got up and sat down again. Would the doctor never come out of there?

This is a good description of temporary restlessness instead of the emotional kind we're after.

> Jeremy cracked his knuckles, an old habit that reappeared whenever he was in this situation. "I don't love you anymore," he said.

Not bad. We have a physical display of restlessness to match his internal restlessness—Jeremy wants out of a relationship. But the act of cracking knuckles is a bit stale. As with pacing, tapping, drumming, biting nails, twirling strands of hair, we need something fresher here.

> Beyond that door sat Mr. Ratner, the man whom Warren hated more than any other living person. Ratner had kept him in this flunky job too long, and Warren was about to do something crazy. But what? Storm in and quit? Simply walk out quietly? All he knew was that he couldn't come in here and sit behind this desk in this cubicle for another day.

This doesn't really convey restlessness. Warren hates his boss and his job, but I don't get the sense of that kinetic energy that restlessness needs. This might work to depict confusion, or any of a variety of other emotions, but not restlessness.

GOOD EXAMPLES

I very much like this description of restlessness in Ann Beattie's short story "Greenwich Time" because it shows physical manifestation of restlessness both in the form of insomnia and in a hunger for motion.

For a long time, he has been thinking about water, about traveling somewhere so that he can walk on the beach, see the ocean. Every year he spends in New York he gets more and more restless. He often wakes up at night in his apartment, hears the air-conditioners roaring and the woman in the apartment above shuffling away her insomnia in satin slippers.

The most restless character I ever created is Libby from my novel *Places to Stay the Night.* Her restlessness as a teenager springs from her unhappiness with life in a small town in western Massachusetts (you can see how I drew from my own life in helping me create that emotion!); her restlessness as an adult comes from her frustration at never having left that small town and her unhappiness with her marriage and her children. First, here is the sixteen-year-old Libby. Notice how her restlessness takes a physical manifestation.

That's when she said it the first time. "I'm getting out of here."

For an instant, Tom thought she meant out of the car. He hadn't even tried to kiss her yet.

"Out of Holly," she said, as if she could read his mind.

"Yeah?" he said. It was a silly notion. They were sixteen years old and there was no place else to go. But he played along.

"I am so sick of all this corn," she moaned, laying her head back on the seat. . . .

"How fast does this go?" she whispered.

Again he was confused. How fast does what go? he thought. . . .

"This," she said, again as if she had read his mind. She patted the top of the stick shift.

"Fast," he whispered back. Steppenwolf was on the radio. Magic Carpet Ride. "Real fast," he said.

"Let's do it," she said.

The adult Libby's physical manifestation of her restlessness is to finally leave, twenty years after the above scene. But the source of her unhappiness is deeper and stronger than the simple boredom of a young girl.

When Libby Holliday finally left her family, she went to Los Angeles, to Hollywood. She did not go to become a movie star.

She was thirty-six years old and her days of becoming a starlet, an ingenue, someone like Sandra Dee in those Tammy movies, were long gone. She went because she thought it was her last chance. Because she thought that if she spent one more day in Holly, Massachusetts, one more day looking at a husband she did not love and two teenage children who frightened her the way strangers in dark shopping mall parking lots frightened her, one more day in that house, that room, that bed, she would certainly shrivel up and die.

EXERCISES

1. We have looked at a lot of clichéd ways to show restlessness through motion (pacing, tapping, etc.). But we've seen a few more interesting ones too, such as a woman described as "shuffling away her insomnia in satin slippers" and a young girl wanting to drive fast in a Firebird. Make a list of other fresh ways to physically portray this kinetic emotion.

Objective: To look beyond the easy and obvious descriptions and find a fresh way to convey the emotion.

2. Look at the list you made for exercise one. Which description best fits a teenager who wants to leave home? Which description best fits an adult who is unhappy with a marriage or love affair? Which best fits someone who, as Eberhardt wrote, "shall always be haunted by thoughts of a sundrenched elsewhere"? Now, write one sentence using both the character and the emotion.

Objective: To remember that emotions must suit the character and that there are different degrees of an emotion.

3. Choose one of the characters from exercise two and the physical manifestation of that person's restlessness from exercise one. Expand them into a one-page character description.

Objective: To show both sides of the emotion of restlessness—the kinetic and the internal—and to explore how that can help you define a character.

REVENGE

We can think of vengeance almost gleefully: Getting revenge—it sounds so sweet! After all, how many times have others hurt us, or betrayed us, or simply done us wrong and we then spend countless hours dreaming up ways to get back at them. Some ways are gory and horrible, some are silly, others are just wicked.

But the emotion of vengeance is a little more complex than that. It has a dark side that shouldn't be ignored. It is, after all, one thing to have a character fantasize about revenge, or to feel vengeful, and quite another to have that character act on those feelings, to actually take revenge. Before you have a character take the air out of her ex-lover's tires because he left her for another woman, consider what that tells your reader about the character. How does that act change the story? The person? The reader's response to both?

Charlotte Brontë describes those two sides of vengeance perfectly in *Jane Eyre*: "Something of vengeance I had tasted for the first time; as aromatic wine it seemed, on swallowing, warm and racy; its afterflavor, metallic and corroding, gave me a sensation as if I had been poisoned."

Here is one emotion that becomes stronger, more complicated, and more intense if you have your character act on it. Is it enough to feel vengeful? Or are you willing to have your character take that next, larger step to action? This emotion should come with a warning label to remind the writer he may be changing the story or character too much by moving that character from feeling to action. Not so with love, surprise, gratitude, suspicion, or dozens of other emotions. The actions with them often follow the feeling logically. A character feels love and then wildly declares it; a character feels surprise and gasps, "Oh!" and so on.

Considering revenge or feeling vengeful is "warm and racy"; but remember that taking revenge leaves the sensation of being poisoned.

BAD EXAMPLES

> Will stabbed the creep two more times, then wiped the blood from the knife on his handkerchief. "That'll show the bastard for double-crossing me," Will said, satisfied. Then he went back to his office to work.

This is an interesting example. If Will is a serial killer or a sociopath, it's probably well done. But if he's supposed to be a sympathetic character, the writer has neglected to even hint at a consequence for his very severe action.

> Susan was going to give him a taste of his own medicine.

Add to this list phrases like "an eye for an eye," "give him his just desserts," "give him what was coming to him," "pay off old scores," "tit for tat," "measure for measure," or any other cliché that simply means getting even. Remember that the emotion of vengefulness is not a simple one. Like all emotions, remember to avoid clichés and to work at getting to the heart of the feeling.

> Aha! Gillian thought, satisfied. She knew exactly how to get back at that worm Evan, to make him feel as low and small as he'd made her feel all these years, screwing other women and stealing her money. She'd sleep with his brother Carl. Also a worm, but this time she had nothing invested except making Evan feel as bad as she did. Gillian put on her best smile, took a swig of her scotch, and sashayed over to Carl. The alarm went off just before her dream got her where she wanted to be. "Damn!" Gillian groaned, hitting the snooze button. But the moment was gone.

Not bad until it turned out to be a dream. Gillian described her feelings well and her revenge seemed almost justified, somewhere in the middle of the emotional spectrum perhaps. But the reader—and Gillian—are deprived of any satisfaction or development by the old device of the dream.

GOOD EXAMPLES

F. Scott Fitzgerald's short story "Bernice Bobs Her Hair" has always been a favorite of mine, not only because of how perfectly it captures the Jazz Age, but also because it has the sweetest revenge scene I know. Bernice is the provincial cousin visiting the glamorous Marjorie. After taking Marjorie's advice on how to be popular, Bernice becomes so popular her cousin schemes to get her to bob her hair, an act that ruins Bernice. Bernice acts on her vengeful feelings at the end, but Fitzgerald has made Marjorie so wicked that the reader is rooting for Bernice and cheers on her revenge.

> She was by the bedside now, very deliberate and calm. She acted swiftly. Bending over she found one of the braids of Marjorie's hair, followed it up with her hand to the point nearest the head, and then holding it a little slack so that the sleeper would feel no pull, she reached down with the shears and severed it. With the pigtail in her hand she held her breath. Marjorie had muttered something in her sleep. Bernice deftly amputated the other braid, paused for a moment, and then flitted swiftly and silently back to her own room.

If "Bernice Bobs Her Hair" is at one end of the spectrum—the end in which the reader wants the protagonist to act—then Walter Kirn's "Thumbsucker" is somewhere in the middle. The protagonist is a thirteen-year-old boy who still sucks his thumb. A hippie dentist named Perry Lyman hypnotizes him and successfully halts the thumbsucking. But as a result, the boy loses the girl he loves, the thumbsucking he loves, and even, he claims, his soul. He knows Lyman's "power animal" is a wolf and uses that secret information to get revenge.

> I signalled Joel to raise the sign I'd made, then broke into a trot along the road. I saw Perry Lyman glance over at the sign and I noticed his front tire wobbling. That's when I started howling. Joel howled, too. The howls came out of me like weird black scarves. They scared me. And they rattled Perry Lyman. He turned and flipped me the bird as he passed, a look of disintegration on his face. He couldn't have known what he'd done to deserve this—the bloody wolf sign and my demented yapping. I knew at that moment I'd broken his power, just as he'd broken mine.

At the opposite end of the spectrum is Susan Power's short story "Red Moccasins." The vengeful feelings come from such a strong place—the death of a woman's child—that the reader understands the horrible act of the protagonist taking another child's life. Yet that "afterflavor, metallic and corroding" that Brontë describes remains in the reader's heart long after the story ends.

> She was wearing the flannel nightdress I'd given her for Christmas, and she was barefoot. She came right up to me. We must dress you, I said, still silent. She was obedient, her eyes glazed and swollen from crying. She lifted her arms so I could remove the nightdress. Her skin shriveled in the cold, but she didn't shiver. I dressed her then, in the trade cloth dress and leggings. I tied the belt around her waist and slipped the cape over her head. I smoothed her thick braids. Finally I knelt before her and fit the beaded moccasins on her feet. I tied the laces.
> "You dance," I hissed. The words were white smoke in the air.

EXERCISES

1. Describe your most delightful revenge fantasy. Why do you want revenge? Who is the person? What horribly wicked things would you like to do? Use strong details and be specific.

Objective: To show that vengefulness can be fun. Thinking about getting revenge is safe and sometimes even satisfying.

2. Now write a scene in which a character actually does what you fantasized about doing. Write it in third person. How does the character feel after he has done the act? How has he changed?

Objective: To show how feeling vengeful and acting on that feeling can change the character and the story.

3. In "Red Moccasins," after the narrator has made Bernadine dance herself to death, she says, " . . . I discovered that magic let loose can take on a life of its own." She then goes on to describe being haunted by Bernadine and deserted by even the magpies. Write a paragraph that describes what happens to your character from exercise two after he lets his magic loose. In other words, what is the result of his action?

Objective: To remind us that vengeance has consequences.

SADNESS

"When you are unhappy or dissatisfied, is there anything in the world more maddening than to be told that you should be contented with your lot?" wrote Kathleen Norris in *Hands Full of Living*. I like that quote because it helps to explain what sadness is: It is unhappiness and dissatisfaction. And it is sometimes present for no good reason that anyone can see. Unlike grief or loss, sadness is not always about death or destruction or disaster. Sometimes it is unexplainable.

I remember a friend of mine bursting into tears one night in a Memphis hotel room where we were staying on vacation. "What's wrong?" I asked her. "I'm just not happy," she said, crying harder. Was it her job? Her boyfriend? Her financial situation? To everything I asked, she answered no. She simply was sad.

The most basic definition of sadness, really, is that it is the opposite of happiness. This is illustrated well by Zora Neale Hurston in *Dust Tracks on a Road* when she writes: "I have been in Sorrow's kitchen and licked out all the pots" and "I have stood on the peaky mountain wrapped in rainbows."

Even though sadness can be defined simply, remember not to underestimate its power over your characters. A character affected by sadness is a character changed. So you cannot treat this emotion too lightly. I like the way L.M. Montgomery describes the effects of sadness on a person in *Anne of Green Gables*: ". . . and no life is ever quite the same again when once that cold, sanctifying touch has been laid upon it."

The biggest pitfall in rendering sadness is to confuse it with unhappiness. Unhappiness is more fleeting and does not run as deep as sadness, which is a larger and more complex emotion. We are unhappy when we miss a phone call we've been anticipating, when we burn our dinner or run late for a meeting. Sadness can be mysteriously pervasive or caused by more important events—death, divorce, missed opportunities—and its effects are both deeper and longer lasting.

BAD EXAMPLES

> Sadness filled Jessie. She looked at the empty house one last time, then slowly drove away.

An easy cop-out for describing emotions is to say this or that "filled" the character. There is some degree of truth and accuracy in that we have all been consumed by grief or passion or happiness or sadness or many other feelings. But it is too easy. It doesn't illuminate anything about the emotion. How does it feel to be filled with sadness? What physical reactions does the sadness create? What gestures does Jessie make in response to—or as a result of—her sadness?

> Kimberly was so sad, all she could do was cry. She cried and cried, and just when she thought she was done, she cried some more.

Again, too easy. Although it's true we often cry—continually, constantly, unstoppably—when we are sad, this doesn't tell us anything new about the emotion itself. Instead, it relies on an easy trigger for the reader: crying equals sadness. And that's not good enough.

> Something was wrong with Fred, but he couldn't put his finger on it. He loved his wife. His job was more than satisfactory. Both of his children seemed happy enough and smart enough and attractive enough to please any parent. Even their new puppy was successfully housebroken. No, Fred thought, nothing to complain about. So what was wrong?

This writer circles the emotion but never lands right on it. Fred might simply be sad, but the writer has left it up to the reader to make that emotional decision.

GOOD EXAMPLES

The narrator in Max Apple's story "Bridging" has become a Girl Scout leader in an effort to help his daughter get over the death of her mother. As the narrator sits with Kay, the other Girl Scout leader, Apple uses common, everyday images to convey sadness, ending with a simile.

> We both think about what might have been as we sit beside her glass coffee pot with our lists of sachet supplies. If she was Barbra Streisand and I Robert Redford and the music started playing in the background to give us a clue and there was a long close-up of our lips, we might just fade into middle age together. . . . When Kay looked at me before going to put alcohol on the mosquito bite, our mutual sadness dripped from us like the last drops of coffee through the grinds.

Jamaica Kincaid describes the expression of sadness in this paragraph from "Xuela." Kincaid's fresh language and keen eye for detail move beyond stereotype. She surprises us by imagining tears as "a new source of water" and with expressions like "my small self."

> . . . it was so intense, so overwhelming, so deep: she grabbed the thick pouch that was her stomach, she pulled at her hair, she pounded her bosom, large tears rolled out of her eyes and down her cheeks, and they came in such profusion that if they had become a new source of water, as in a myth or a fairy tale, my small self would not have been surprised.

A wonderful example of how sadness is simply the opposite of happiness, of how it often comes from no particular loss or disaster, of its inexplicable nature can be found in Elizabeth McCracken's novel *The Giant's House: A Romance.*

> I am a fundamentally sad person, a fundamentally unlovable person, a person who spends her life longing for a number of things she cannot bring herself to name or define.

EXERCISES

1. Sadness and crying are linked in our minds. Choose a character, say a thirty-year-old single woman in Boston, or one of your own. Decide she is sad. Nothing in particular has happened. Rather, she is just overcome by sadness. Write a scene that does not use crying as

an expression of her sadness. Give the reader fresh images and fresh language to truly evoke the emotion.

Objective: To try to move beyond the stereotypes associated with emotions.

2. In the description from Kincaid's story "Xuela," the character does cry. Using the same character from exercise one, now write a scene in which crying *is* an expression of her sadness.

Objective: To write an emotion, in a scene that demands a stereotype, using a fresh eye, fresh language, and a new way.

3. When sadness strikes and it is not linked to a specific event or person, it is difficult to explain. You've already seen how McCracken attempts to describe such a feeling. Here is another: "Other people's happiness is always a bore. It sucks the oxygen out of the room; you're left gasping, greedy, amazed by a deficit in yourself you hadn't even noticed." Now you try to explain that emotion of sadness. You might have to make several attempts before you get one that rings true.

Objective: To describe an emotion that is not linked to something concrete; you can't rely on reaction or easy association.

SHAME

Shame is a strong and painful emotion. It has a feeling all its own—and a powerful one. Do not confuse it with embarrassment. Once, when my editor and her husband took my soon-to-be husband and me out for dinner, I knocked a glass of wine in my fiancé's lap. What I felt then was embarrassment. Or when I walked in on the little old man using the airplane lavatory without locking the door behind him. We both felt embarrassed, but certainly not shamed. In both examples I made a mistake, but I hadn't done anything truly wrong. Neither episode was going to keep me awake at night or make me flinch at the memory. People would not think less of me—nor I of myself—as a result of these incidents.

Shame is caused by harsher emotions—guilt, unworthiness, even disgrace. It can create physical pain or make us twitch or blush in anguish. These reactions make it a difficult emotion to conceal.

Have you ever been caught shoplifting? Cheating on your lover? Cheating on a test? Have you ever had to call someone to get you out of jail? To put you in a rehab center? To drive you home because you totalled the car, drunk? Have you ever wanted to hide from your parents? Your childhood home? Your unemployment check? Your too-small winter coat? Your shoes with the holes in the bottoms? Then you know shame. No matter how carefully we live our lives, we all have felt shame at some point. And it may be the worst feeling in the entire spectrum of emotions, because it makes us feel worthless and utterly alone, as if no one else feels this way and as if we are not even worthy of someone else's comfort.

People ask, "Have you no shame?" when you bring dishonor or condemnation to yourself or your family or friends. Shame has within it disappointment—in ourselves or our surroundings or the lives we are leading. It does not, however, include hopelessness. Unlike despair, shame does not feel permanent. We can change our circumstances or our environment; we can seek forgiveness; we can accept that which caused us shame, or which shamed us.

When writing about shame, keep the nature of the emotion in mind. Remember how it feels. Or remember how inconsolable a friend felt when you were trying to help them through a time of shame. If you include hope as part of shame, don't neglect the painfulness of the emotion. Without that, you are not conveying the essence of it.

BAD EXAMPLES

Sally-Anne blushed. How would she ever recover from this?

Although we don't see what the "this" is, blushing is a response to embarrassment, not shame. Shame runs much deeper than reddened cheeks. Even if the thing that caused her to blush is actually shameful, the writer has chosen the wrong way to illustrate shame.

Even though Harrison dressed hurriedly and managed to get the woman out the window before his wife burst in, he still couldn't stop laughing at how close he'd come to getting caught.

Harrison does not feel shame; he feels relief, perhaps even smugness, at getting away with his infidelity. Remember that there is deep pain in shame and that there is a clear recognition that we have done something wrong or are in some way inadequate. Harrison's glee at his escape suggests he doesn't recognize that he is doing something wrong.

Wendy still felt embarrassed when she drove past her childhood home. She lived on the other side of town now, in a new subdivision where all the houses sparkled inside and out.

This has great potential for conveying shame, even though the writer chooses the word *embarrassed* to describe how Wendy feels. Shifting the focus to the new houses lessens the power of Wendy's shame. Concrete details about her childhood home would make a stronger point: What about it shamed Wendy?

GOOD EXAMPLES

I cannot think of a better active example of shame than this one from Junot Díaz's short story "How to Date a Brown Girl (black girl, white girl, or halfie)." The selection of shameful details, such as "the government cheese" and "embarrassing photos of your family in the *campo*," make the emotion come to life. But perhaps the real strength is that Díaz manages to convey shame so effectively without ever mentioning the emotion.

> Clear the government cheese from the refrigerator. If the girl's from the Terrace, stack the boxes in the crisper. If she's from the Park or Society Hill, then hide the cheese in the cabinet above the oven, where she'll never see it. Leave a reminder under your pillow to get out the cheese before morning or your moms will kick your ass. Take down any embarrassing photos of your family in the *campo*, especially that one with the half-naked kids dragging a goat on a rope. Hide the picture of yourself with an Afro. Make sure the bathroom is presentable. Since your toilet can't flush toilet paper, put the bucket with all the crapped on toilet paper under the sink. Spray the bucket with Lysol, then close the lid.

Patricia Henley describes not just shame, but also its effect on her later in life in her story "The Secret of Cartwheels." Her list of small things that never matched brings her shame into sharp focus, again showing the power of concrete details.

> When I remember those years at home, this is one of the things I focus on: how nothing ever matched—not sheets, not barrettes, not cups and saucers, not socks. And sometimes I think the sad and petty effort to have matching things has been one of the chief concerns of my adult life.

In "Bless Me, Father, for I Have Sinned," Ray Bradbury shows us the shame a man feels over beating his beloved dog years earlier; but then Bradbury goes on to the next step—forgiveness. After you read the example below, look at the example from the same story in the section on forgiveness.

> Who was he? A beast, an animal, a dog, my love. And he looked at me with such great dark eyes that it locked my heart and it's been locked forever after with shame. I could not then forgive myself. All these years, the memory of my love and how I failed him, and every Christmas since, not the rest of the year, but

every Christmas Eve, his ghost comes back, I see the dog, I
hear the beating, I know my failure, Oh, God!

EXERCISES

1. Junot Díaz depicts shame by showing us all the things the narrator wants to hide from girls he aims to impress. The government
cheese and crapped on toilet paper are painful reminders of this boy's
shame. Write a two-page scene, in the second person, that is basically
a list of what a character is hiding to impress someone. It could be a
rich boy hiding material things from a poorer boy he wants as a friend.
It could be a married man hiding signs of his wife from a woman he
wants to seduce. It could be an alcoholic hiding signs of her drinking
from her adult son. Or choose a character and setting of your own.

Objective: To demonstrate concrete details to illustrate shame.

2. Choose one source of shame (like Patricia Henley's mismatched
items). Then write a two-page scene in which an adult character is
still haunted by that shameful thing.

Objective: To demonstrate the effects of shame through character
development.

3. First, write a scene in which a character confesses a shameful
act to another character, in the way the man in Ray Bradbury's story
admits to a priest that he beat his dog. Then write a scene in which
the character finds forgiveness for that act (as in Bradbury's example
under "Forgiveness"). Finally, connect the two scenes so they shape
a story. How does the character move from shame to the climax of
forgiveness?

Objective: To take a character through an arc of emotional growth.

SURPRISE

Every time I write the word *surprise*, I feel like I should add three or four exclamation points after it. I picture a dark room and a bunch of people in silly hats hiding, then the room coming ablaze with light and all the people jumping out yelling, "Surprise!!!!" But this doesn't make it an emotion to overlook here, or in our fiction.

In writing fiction, we can use surprise in so many interesting ways that we have to almost banish the above description from our writing minds. The emotion of surprise is what we feel when we are caught unaware—by guests at a surprise party, yes, but also by guns in our backs, a mouse skittering across the floor, a bloody nose, a dead body, a bat in the bedroom, the enemy troops coming over the hill.

Surprise isn't always good. It's walking in the front door and discovering a burglar. It's the Dear John letter found on the kitchen table. Capturing how a character feels in that instant is more challenging than the word itself might imply. As a writer trying to convey surprise, your job becomes one of paring down to an instant. Surprise isn't long-lasting, yet its intensity is worthy of getting just right. You must, therefore, rely on setting and plot and character to buoy the effectiveness of the moment of surprise. Everything must be in place so the reader feels it along with the character.

The verb *surprise* means to fill a person with wonder or disbelief. But the emotion of surprise refers to the reaction to what is unexpected or unusual. Not as strong as wonder, nor as emphatic as astonishment or amazement, surprise should be used sparingly and with accuracy, only when your character is caught unaware.

Perhaps it is best to take Alice Walker's advice. In her poem "Expect Nothing," she writes: "Expect nothing. Live frugally / On surprise." If we write surprise frugally, we are more likely to get it right.

BAD EXAMPLES

> "Yikes!" Billy cried. "You scared the bejesus out of me!"

Alfred Hitchcock once said that he could scare any moviegoer by having a character in a film walk into a room and have a cat jump on his back. That kind of surprise, demonstrated above, isn't emotional. You can always have a character react to being startled. But you have to work harder to have it matter.

> Gayle was surprised that James was so late. He was usually punctual, early even. She began to imagine catastrophes—car wrecks, brain tumors, space invasions.

I actually like the example above a lot for character development. But the emotion of surprise isn't what's being conveyed here. Worry, maybe. Or fear. But just using the word *surprised* isn't necessarily evoking it.

> "Mary Dingle?" the young man at Mary's door said politely. Mary nodded.
> "I'm your son. The one you gave birth to in 1959 and handed over to the Murphys." The young man smiled and extended his hand.
> "Nice to meet you," Mary said.

Phew! This is certainly a setup for conveying surprise. But the writer misses the opportunity!

GOOD EXAMPLES

In "The Jilting of Granny Weatherall," Katherine Anne Porter uses an unlikely event to show surprise: death. Granny's description captures the essence of surprise: "I wasn't even thinking about it."

> So, my dear Lord, this is my death and I wasn't even thinking about it. My children have come to see me die. But I can't, it's not time. Oh, I always hated surprises.

Laura Kasischke shows surprise through the character's reactions rather than thoughts. The narrator of the novel *Suspicious River* is a prostitute. Here she has just received money from a man she's about to have sex with.

I looked at the money in my hand. Two twenties. Two tens. I slipped my foot out of my shoe and bent a bit to slip the bills in under my heel.

The slap surprised me as I was standing up again, lifting my eyes back toward him.

We were both still smiling.

Just the flat surface of his hand made contact with my face, and it knocked me off balance. He stood in the same place, looking.

I hadn't wanted to gasp, but I knew I had by the way he laughed, that smirk, at my shocked face. It stung. It must've gone very red, burning, or drywall white. Then he hit me again.

In my opinion, Alice Walker's short story "The Flowers" is as near to perfect as a short story can be—and it's only two pages long. One of the many things Walker does well is evoke surprise. The story is about a ten-year-old girl named Myop, out for a walk on a summer day, picking flowers. The following passage is what happens to her, the surprise she feels. Many writers would have ended the story on that emotional pitch. But Walker takes it beyond surprise, using that emotion as a springboard to other, larger issues and emotion.

Myop began to circle back to the house, back to the peacefulness of the morning. It was then she stepped smack into his eyes. Her heel became lodged in the broken ridge between brow and nose, and she reached down quickly, unafraid, to free herself. It was only when she saw his naked grin that she gave a little yelp of surprise.

EXERCISES

1. Katherine Anne Porter uses death as a vehicle to bring surprise. Write a short scene (no more than half a page) using surprise for each of these three events: giving birth, a thunderstorm, love at first sight.

Objective: To practice using surprise in scenes that take people unaware.

2. Porter uses an interior response—the character's thoughts—to surprise; Kasischke uses an external response—gasping, getting knocked off balance, smiling. Write a scene in which a character gets

deliberately hit in the face by a Frisbee thrown by her teenage son. In the scene, only use interior responses. Then write a second scene in which the same thing happens but this time only use exterior responses.

Objective: To practice both ways—interior and exterior—to illustrate surprise.

3. This one takes a little research. Read the Alice Walker story "The Flowers." You can find it in the collection *In Love and Trouble: Stories of Black Women*. Once you've read it and seen where Myop's surprise of stepping into that skull led her and the story, analyze how Walker used the emotion to move to larger themes. Write your thoughts on paper. What are the themes of the story? What does Myop learn after her "surprise"? What does the last line of the story mean?

Objective: To learn from the masters. As writers, we have the best teachers available on library shelves. Study and analyze what they've done well.

SUSPICION

My mother tells a story of her old friend Catherine who, as a young newlywed, discovered that her husband was cheating on her with a woman who rented their lake house that winter. The young husband promised Catherine he would never see the woman again. The woman moved from the lake house, somewhere out of state. Catherine and her husband went on to have four children and to be married over forty years. In her sixties now, she recently asked my mother if she remembered the story of the husband's infidelity.

My mother had assumed that Catherine and her husband had put the affair far behind them. We did, I suppose, Catherine said. But even though he has never again given me reason to suspect him of cheating, I've lived my whole life suspecting that very thing.

In *Middlemarch*, George Eliot asks: "What loneliness is more lonely than distrust?" Suspicion is distrust, but often without proof or evidence. A character might be suspicious of a stranger, of a promise, of a situation. Catherine's distrust of her husband was all based on events that happened four decades ago.

But you must be careful not to have a character's suspicious feelings come from nowhere. Then you risk creating a character who appears to be paranoid, or worse. It is true we often feel suspicious for reasons that are unclear to us, but in fiction, the reader must buy into the character's emotion.

Remember, too, that suspicion can be small—a nagging feeling, a minor detail that a character can't let go of, a phrase that doesn't sound quite right. Or, it can be large—drawers that have been gone through, a spouse who doesn't come home one night.

To write suspicion believably, you must make the reader understand the source of the character's distrust, even if it is simply that she distrusts men with moustaches. Or, like Catherine, that an old wound never completely healed.

BAD EXAMPLES

> Linnea held the love letter in her hand, almost triumphantly. She was right! Artie and Roberta had been seeing each other behind her back. She wasn't such a fool after all.

Here, Linnea's suspicions have been confirmed. We don't understand the emotion of suspicion as a result of this. Instead, we see satisfaction, perhaps, in being proven right.

> Peter sniffed at Rachel's sleeping form beside him. Old Spice. He recognized the smell. How closely was she working with Jon tonight? When he called their office, he only got voice mail. And why had she thrown her clothes in the wash, herself into that hot bubble bath, as soon as she got home?

This gives us good, solid reasons for Peter to feel suspicious. But it doesn't give us any insight into the emotion. The situation is cliché, and therefore it comes across as too facile. He has evidence, certainly. But what does he feel?

> Celia's big sister Peggy had warned her not to talk to strangers, especially men strangers. Especially men strangers with moustaches. Still, Celia moved toward the man when he motioned to her, his moustache bobbing up and down comically.

This is a suspicious situation. But Celia doesn't feel suspicious so the author avoids confronting the emotion.

GOOD EXAMPLES

Boo Radley, the Finch's mysterious neighbor in Harper Lee's *To Kill a Mockingbird*, fills Scout with fear and dread and curiosity. So much so that at the novel's start, the Radley place has its own mythology, which captures the suspicious feelings of a child:

> Inside the house lived a malevolent phantom. People said he existed, but Jem and I had never seen him. People said he went out at night when the moon was down, and peeped in windows. When people's azaleas froze in a cold snap, it was because he had breathed on them. Any stealthy crimes committed in Maycomb were his work. Once the town was terrorized by a series of morbid nocturnal events: people's chickens

and household pets were found mutilated; although the culprit was Crazy Addie, who eventually drowned himself in Barker's Eddy, people still looked at the Radley Place, unwilling to discard their initial suspicions. A Negro would not pass the Radley Place at night, he would cut across to the sidewalk opposite and whistle as he walked. The Maycomb school grounds adjoined the back of the Radley lot; from the Radley chickenyard tall pecan trees shook their fruit into the schoolyard, but the nuts lay untouched by the children: Radley pecans would kill you.

Constantia and Josephine, two sisters in Katherine Mansfield's story "The Daughters of the Late Colonel," are suspicious of their sister, Kate. Constantia cannot decide if she trusts Kate; Mansfield uses voice and interior monologue to explore suspicion.

The whole difficulty was to prove anything. How did one prove things, how could one? Suppose Kate had stood in front of her and deliberately made a face. Mightn't she very well have been in pain? Wasn't it impossible, at any rate, to ask Kate if she was making a face at her? If Kate answered "No"—and of course she would say "No"— what a position! How undignified! Then again Constantia suspected, she was almost certain that Kate went to her chest of drawers when she and Josephine were out, not to take things but to spy.

Tim O'Brien gives voice to suspicion in his novel *In the Lake of the Woods*. When John Wade returns from Vietnam he already feels cut off emotionally from his girlfriend, Kathy. Rather than confront her, John spies on her, suspicious that she is with another man. Look at how O'Brien addresses the ambiguity of the emotion:

He stationed himself at a bus stop outside. His eyes ached— his heart, too—everything. And there was also the squeeze of indecision. At times he was struck by a fierce desire to believe that the suspicion was nothing but a demon in his head. Other times he wanted to believe the worst. He didn't know why. It was as though something inside him, his genes or his bone marrow, required the certainty of a confirmed betrayal: a witnessed kiss, a witnessed embrace. The facts would be absolute. In a dim way, only half admitted, John understood that the alternative was simply to love her, and to go on loving her, yet somehow the ambiguity seemed intolerable. Nothing could ever be sure, not if he spied forever, because there was always the threat of tomorrow's treachery, or next year's treachery, or the treachery implicit in all the tomorrows beyond that.

EXERCISES

1. Reread the excerpt from *To Kill a Mockingbird* in which Scout describes how suspicion takes shape in a child's mind. Of course, childish suspicions can be outlandish; the authenticity comes from the authority with which the child tells the story. That authority is achieved several ways. The child speaks with certainty. Also, the story is crammed with details and facts. Finally, the words used are true to a child's voice. With this in mind, write a one-page description of something or someone a child is suspicious of. Be sure to write it in the first person and stick to a child's point of view.

Objective: To practice writing emotion in a child's point of view.

2. Later in the Mansfield story, we learn that Constantia set traps to catch Kate in the act of spying. Constantia arranged things in her drawer in a special order and then checked to see if anything was displaced. Write a scene in which a suspicious character sets a trap for another character. Be as imaginative as you can. For example, how would one lover who suspects another lover of cheating try to catch him?

Objective: To use action to illustrate the emotion of suspicion.

3. Tim O'Brien describes the emotion of suspicion as "the threat of tomorrow's treachery." John Wade is not unlike my mother's friend Catherine. Write a paragraph in first person in which a character describes that same feeling of suspicion. Why is she suspicious in the first place? What does it feel like? John Wade spies on Kathy; how does your character act on her emotion? Be sure not to resolve the feeling. John Wade talks about "the treachery implicit in all the tomorrows beyond that."

Objective: To give a voice to the emotion of suspicion.

SYMPATHY

Sympathy is a dangerous emotion to write. Does this surprise you? Perhaps you are imagining already all of the horrible fictional twists and character flaws and tragedies that can elicit sympathy: Death. Destruction. Heartache. Pain.

But, as Selma Lagerlöf wrote in *The General's Ring*: "Even the little pigs grunt when the old boar suffers." In other words, for our purposes of learning to write emotions well, it's almost too easy to write sympathy in the face of such large fictional events as death and destruction. We are in danger of ending up with melodrama: characters running about, wringing their hands, fretting, voicing clichés.

The second worst thing we end up with is sentimentality. Characters feel so much sympathy for their fellow characters that their world is reduced to a giant romance novel. In general, people are *un*sympathetic; when we try to force sympathy from a character, we often end up with sentimentality instead.

Yet sympathy is a real and important emotion. We will inevitably find ourselves faced with having to write it, and to write it well. The best way I can come up with to practice doing that is to examine more basic reasons for sympathy before we tackle it on a large scale. If you can make a character show sympathy over the loss of someone's tomato plants in a frost, and then over the death of a family dog, and do them convincingly, perhaps you are then ready to tackle the larger tragedies.

Years ago, in Barcelona, I visited the Picasso Museum. As I wandered through the building, admiring the still lifes and nudes, I kept wondering where all the Picassos were. And then an English-speaking visitor explained it to me: These were all Picassos, done while he was a student there. In other words, Picasso didn't begin by inventing Cubism. He first had to study and experiment with the same ordinary forms every painter begins with.

That is, I think, the best approach for writing sympathy well too. Let's look at it and practice it on a simpler level so we can avoid melodrama and sentimentality. At its simplest, sympathy is what Simone Weil wrote in *Waiting for God*: "The love of our neighbor in all of its fullness simply means being able to say to him, 'What are you going through?' "

BAD EXAMPLES

> They all stood awkwardly in front of Miles, uncertain what to say or how to say it. He was one of them—a child, really. But with this tragedy he had started down a different, more adult path, a place where they would all travel someday, some distant, far-off day, a place where they did not yet want to venture. To touch him, to reach out to him, might bring them closer to where he now stood, alone, parentless, homeless, at sea. "Sorry," they each mumbled in turn. "So sorry."

This shifts to melodrama at a certain point. Perhaps it is simply too overwritten to avoid melodrama. The theme addressed is certainly meaningful and one that would evoke sympathy. But the writer goes overboard.

We've all heard platitudes used too often in both life and fiction.

> "If there's anything I can do . . ."

> "God has his reasons."

> "He's with God now."

> "I'm sorry."

This list could go on and on. If you want to show a character speaking in clichés, use one of these. But if you really want to show sympathy, avoid them!

> "We all loved Margaret. You know that. We can only hope she's happy now, in heaven, looking down at all of us and smiling." The thought comforted Jim. For the first time since he got the news, he smiled too.

Here's a good example of sympathy turned into sentimentality. Would the sentiments the speaker expressed really comfort Jim? I don't think so. This is pseudosympathy, and it works too quickly and easily.

GOOD EXAMPLES

You've Got to Read This is a collection of stories that most impressed and inspired contemporary fiction writers. The writers provide introductory essays to the stories they selected. I was struck by what Amy Tan wrote in her essay preceding the story "Pie Dance" by Molly Giles. The story is told by an ex-wife about her relationship with her husband's new wife. "Curiously," Tan points out, "she has enough sympathy for the new wife to want to tell her 'who among us is perfect, Pauline.'"

> She favors what the magazines call the "layered look"—I suspect because she is ashamed of her bottom. She has thin shoulders but a heavy bottom. Well, I want to tell her, who is not ashamed of their bottom. If not their bottom their thighs or their breasts or their wobbly female bellies; who among us is perfect, Pauline.

The narrator in Jamaica Kincaid's story "Song of Roland" is a confident woman who is in love with Roland, a married man whose wife had a list of names of women he had seduced. This fact doesn't bother the narrator; she loves Roland, for now. At this point in the story, the narrator has just gotten her period and, as always, is overjoyed at its arrival. Roland doesn't understand why she doesn't want to bear his children. She is sympathetic to his confusion.

> When I saw him like that, on his face a look that was a mixture—confusion, dumbfoundedness, defeat—I felt much sorrow for him, for his life was reduced to a list of names that were not countries, and to the number of times he brought the monthly flow to a halt; his life was reduced to women, some of them beautiful, wearing dresses made from yards of cloth he had surreptitiously removed from the bowels of the ships where he worked as a stevedore.

I like the way Scout covers up her sympathy for her first grade teacher, Miss Caroline, in *To Kill a Mockingbird* after she loses control of the class. Scout has repeatedly gotten in trouble all morning and is angry at Miss Caroline. But we see a crack of sympathy here despite her denial. Having a character deny sympathy is a good way to avoid the pitfalls of melodrama and sentimentality.

My sojourn in the corner was a short one. Saved by the bell, Miss Caroline watched the class file out for lunch. As I was the last to leave, I saw her sink down into her chair and bury her head in her arms. Had her conduct been more friendly toward me, I would have felt sorry for her. She was a pretty little thing.

EXERCISES

1. Have a character express sympathy for a seemingly small loss, such as one from this list.
- an old pet dies
- a child's favorite doll is lost
- a car is stolen
- due to a blizzard, someone can't make it home for Christmas
- a high school senior does not get into the college of her choice

Write the expression as dialogue. Remember to avoid cliché, sentimentality and melodrama. Once you're done, read out loud what you've written. Does it ring true? If not, try again.

Objective: To practice writing true expressions of sympathy.

2. Scout gives us clues to the fact that she does feel some sympathy toward Miss Caroline in her choice of words: "pretty little thing," "sink down," "bury her head." Write a one-page scene in which a character feels sympathy for another character even though she doesn't want to. Don't use the word *sympathy* or even *sorry*, but clue the reader in to the character's true feelings with other word choices.

Objective: To practice portraying emotions through denial.

3. In "Pie Dance," Molly Giles expresses sympathy for her husband's new wife while also expressing sympathy for all women who are ashamed of some part of their bodies: thighs, breasts, bellies. Choose a general category of people: men, lawyers, widows, redheads, the unemployed, single parents, pregnant women, or one of your own. Write a one-page, first-person narration by someone from that group. Address it to another member of that group who is less insightful, less sympathetic. End the narration with a realization ("who among us is perfect, Pauline") that shows sympathy for the individual as well as for everyone in that group.

Objective: To begin to move beyond a basic expression of sympathy to a larger one.

TENDERNESS

Tenderness is, perhaps, the gentlest of emotions. Therefore, it must be rendered with a light touch. It calls to mind the ways in which a mother handles her newborn, or the look that passes between a long-married couple. We think of fragile things such as a tender petal; of things with a delicate quality like a tender song; of youth or vulnerability as when we say someone is at a tender age; of softness conveyed by a tender heart.

Thesauruses and dictionaries practically float with definitions and synonyms for tenderness: "a soft place in one's heart," my *Roget's* explains. It seems, therefore, that the danger with conveying tenderness is to be too sentimental. It is like walking a balance beam: On one side you fall into sentimental muck; on the other you lose the gentleness necessary to convince your reader.

This is not to say you must only choose soft adjectives or misty verbs. In fact, contrasting the gentleness of the emotion with harder realities is perhaps the best way to truly show tenderness. Or you must find new gentle phrases to convey the emotion without sounding overly sentimental.

Tenderness implies something almost tactile. We say a bruise feels tender. Keeping this in mind is a good way to push yourself toward rendering this emotion effectively. Use physical expressions to show tenderness. Again, be wary of cliché. A soft touch, a hand pressed against a cheek are certainly signs of tenderness, but how much more interesting to show a man washing his lover's hair or bringing her a cup of tea.

BAD EXAMPLES

> She softly touched her baby's [husband's, dying mother's, sleeping child's] cheek.

Soft touches are a predictable way to illustrate tenderness. The challenge is how to do it in a fresh way.

> "Oh, I love you," he whispered tenderly.

Too obvious! Need I say more?

> Looking down at his newborn daughter, Jim's heart actually seemed to swell and grow soft.

This writer is trying to convey a difficult feeling, but the setup is too cliché. The challenge here is to introduce something different and new to convey the emotion or let the scene speak for itself.

GOOD EXAMPLES

In her story "Shiloh," Bobbie Ann Mason creates a tender portrait of a doomed relationship by using lists that suggest the couple's very different interests.

> Norma Jean works at the Rexall drugstore, and she has acquired an amazing amount of information about cosmetics. When she explains to Leroy the three stages of complexion care, involving creams, toners, and moisturizers, he thinks happily of other petroleum products—axle grease, diesel fuel. This is a connection between him and Norma Jean.

Andre Dubus uses the cliché of touching a cheek but transcends trite writing by elevating the language and emotion. In his story "At Night," a wife wakes to find her husband has died. She touches his cheek, but that tender act leads her to explore all of the emotions of death and love, as if the touch is an emotional catalyst.

> But on the summer night when he died while she slept, probably while he slept, too, she woke in the cool dark, the windows open and a pale light in the sky, and the birds singing and she knew before she turned to him, and she did not think of her children, or of being alone. She rolled towards him and touched his face, and her love went out of her, and into his cooling skin, and she wept for what it had done to him, crept up and taken him while he slept and dreamed. Maybe it came out of a dream and the dream became it. Wept, lying on her side, with her hand on his cheek, because he had been alone with it, sur-

prised, maybe confused now as he wandered while the birds sang, seeing the birds, seeing her lying beside his flesh, touching his cheek, saying: "Oh, hon—"

Gabriel García Márquez juxtaposes the painful and horrible with tenderness in his short story "One of These Days."

It was a lower wisdom tooth. The dentist spread his feet and grasped the tooth with the hot forceps. The Mayor seized the arms of the chair, braced his feet with all his strength, and felt an icy void in his kidneys, but didn't make a sound. The dentist moved only his wrist, without rancor, rather with a bitter tenderness, and he said:

"Now you'll pay for our twenty dead men."

EXERCISES

The juxtaposition of something harsh with a tender moment is a wonderful way to show the emotion without sounding cliché or sentimental. Mason uses a tangible contrast—complexion care items with axle grease and fuel oil. Dubus uses a contrast of love and death. And Márquez contrasts pain with "bitter tenderness." All three exercises below ask you to try this approach.

1. Choose two opposite items (complexion cream and axle grease, leather and lace, stone and paper, bricks and straw). Exactly imitate the excerpt from "Shiloh": _____ works at _____ and he/she has acquired an amazing amount of information about _____. When he/she explains to _____ the stages of _____, he/she thinks happily of _____. This is a connection between him/her and _____.

2. One of the ways Dubus manages to convey tenderness while avoiding sentimentality is to use intrusion from the outside world: Singing birds are mentioned twice. Write a one-page scene in which someone is touching someone else's cheek. But twice have an intrusion from the outside world, such as a car alarm sounding, road construction noises, neighbors arguing, or any one you can think of.

3. What is the most physically painful thing you can imagine? Childbirth? Amputation without anesthesia? Describe the process tenderly.

Objective: To learn from good examples.

WORRY

If I were to list all the things I worry about, you might conclude that I am filled with anxiety, a person who could easily and justifiably be labelled a worrywart. I worry about the sale of my books, the careers of my most promising students; I worry about getting writer's block; I worry that my children will behave badly, or get sick, or be unhappy; I worry about money and love and safety; I worry that my car will break down, my hard drive will get erased, my check won't arrive; I worry about large things like fatal diseases striking and world peace and smaller things like a new recipe working out and the moving men arriving on time. Even as I sit here right now I worry that hurricane Bertha is going to hit, that my husband will be late to take our sitter to her bus, that I won't be ready when it's time to leave for vacation tomorrow.

Still, despite all of the above, I really am not a "worrywart." I hardly ever lose sleep over any of these things. I don't bite my nails or twitch or drum my fingers across tabletops. But from time to time, in the course of a day or a week or a month, one or several or many of these things trouble me. And really that's what worry is: to feel uneasy or concerned or threatened by something.

What worry isn't is an obsessive fear: Aliens are going to land, nuclear war is imminent. A worried person might take moderate precautions against her concerns, but she isn't going to build a hideout shelter in her basement and move into it. Worry isn't even fear at all. Instead, it's that nagging feeling in your gut: It's midnight and Grace isn't home yet; I hope she's okay. But you don't put out an APB, or get hysterical, or even start calling emergency rooms yet. You might pace, try to read a magazine, stand by the window, even call her friend to see if she's made it home yet.

The biggest risk in trying to express worry in your writing is to overwrite it, to veer into some other, larger, more extreme emotion.

Remember to keep your characters out of the fallout shelter and simply by the window looking out, fingers crossed.

BAD EXAMPLES

> The news on the TV was bad: China had nuclear weapons. Surely, Elspeth thought as she listened to Tom Brokaw, the U.S. was its perfect target. She thought of all those pictures of Hiroshima she'd seen and she began to tremble. That was her future. And Joey's. And Hank's. Hadn't Nostradamus predicted this very end?

This is a good example of taking worry too far. Instead of worry, the writer has expressed fear, perhaps even despair. Elspeth's reaction is what goes overboard. The setup itself could have led to worry.

> Celeste shook with worry.
> Celeste tapped her foot, worrying.
> Celeste paced.

Too easy! Remember Carol Bly's advice in part one: Try to write the second thing that comes into your mind, not the easy, first thing.

> When the phone rang, Rebecca paused, worried. Who could be calling so early in the morning? "Hello?" she said, picking it up.

This writer skirts dealing with the emotion. I believe Rebecca—or anyone—might be worried if the phone rang at the crack of dawn (we don't even know how early it is!). But how does her worry express itself? What does she think? Or what does she do?

GOOD EXAMPLES

Ernest Hemingway shows worry in the female character in his short story "Hills Like White Elephants," but never uses the word *worry*. He also does not have any descriptions of action and instead relies wholly on dialogue. A couple is sitting, waiting for a train that will take the woman to a place where she will get an abortion. Here is a small piece of that dialogue between the man and woman. She speaks first.

> "And if I don't do it you'll be happy and things will be like they were and you'll love me?"

"I love you now. You know I love you."

"I know. But if I do it, then it will be nice again if I say things are like white elephants, and you'll like it?"

As the character of Neil in David Leavitt's story "Territory" waits for his lover to arrive at Neil's mother's house, he is gripped by worry. Leavitt uses a device of questions that Neil poses to himself to convey his worry. The questions begin as practical ones, then become larger.

> He stands, and the dogs circle him, looking up at his face expectantly. He feels renewed terror at the thought that Wayne will be here soon: Will they sleep in the same room? Will they make love? He has never had sex in his parents' house. How can he be expected to be a lover here, in this place of his childhood, of his earliest shame, in this household of mothers and dogs?

A terrific way to show worry—or any emotion—is to use distraction, to have the character not think about the feeling. This is what Roddy Doyle does in this excerpt from his novel *Paddy Clarke Ha Ha Ha*. Paddy is getting examined by a nurse, and the boys are all worried that she will lift their "mickey" up with an ice-pop stick.

> She was still there. Bent down looking at it. Staring. Maybe rubbing her chin. Making her mind up. There was a cobweb in the corner over the doctor, a big dry one. There was a thread of it swinging. There was a breeze up there. She was making her mind up. If it was bad enough to lift to see the other side. If I didn't look she wouldn't do it. I was looking for the spider. If she did it I'd be finished forever. The most amazing things about spiders was the way they made their webs. I'd never be normal again . . .

EXERCISES

1. In a way, Doyle is spinning a web with his language, showing worry by interspersing Paddy's thoughts with his distraction (the spider) and his concern (the ice-pop stick). Decide on a worry: Will I make my plane? Do I need surgery? Is late Grace all right? Now decide on a distraction: a song on the radio, a magazine article about liposuction, the ticking of a clock. Or choose your own worry and distraction.

Write the final moments before the worry is resolved. Have your character's thoughts move between the concern and the distraction.

Objective: To practice working with distraction as a way to express worry—or any other emotion a character wants to avoid thinking about.

2. Choose a worry that involves two people. Are their amniocentesis results going to be all right? Does their only car need a new transmission? Is the bank foreclosing on their house? Or think of one of your own. Write a half page of dialogue between the two people in which they never actually say they are worried and never say what the problem is. Yet, the reader must leave the dialogue understanding both.

Objective: To practice writing good dialogue and to use dialogue to express an emotion.

3. Think of an awkward situation. A teenager is about to show her mother her pierced navel. Or a man is about to propose to a woman he hardly knows. Or a man leaving his wife is about to tell their son. Or choose one of your own. Now write a series of five questions the character asks himself as he waits. Let the first three be practical. Then let the final two be larger questions that reveal something about the character, the situation, and the relationship between the two people.

Objective: To push worry beyond the practical to the universal so the reader gains a larger insight into character or theme.

ABOUT THE AUTHOR

Ann Hood is the author of six novels, all published by Bantam/Doubleday, including *Somewhere off the Coast of Maine*, *Places to Stay the Night* and *The Properties of Water*. Her short stories and essays have appeared in STORY, *Glimmer Train*, *The New York Times*, *The Washington Post*, *Redbook* and other publications. She has served on the faculty of many universities and writers conferences and presently teaches at New York University. She lives in Providence with her husband and their two children.

INDEX